TEXTUAL SCHOLAR
MAKING OF THE NI

CW01084456

Textual Scholarship and the Making of the New Testament

THE LYELL LECTURES

OXFORD

TRINITY TERM 2011

DAVID C. PARKER

OXFORD
UNIVERSITY PRESS

OXFORD
UNIVERSITY PRESS

Great Clarendon Street, Oxford, OX2 6DP,
United Kingdom

Oxford University Press is a department of the University of Oxford.
It furthers the University's objective of excellence in research, scholarship,
and education by publishing worldwide. Oxford is a registered trade mark of
Oxford University Press in the UK and in certain other countries

First Edition published in 2012

First published in paperback 2014

Published in the United States of America by Oxford University Press
198 Madison Avenue, New York, NY 10016, United States of America

British Library Cataloguing in Publication Data
Data available

Library of Congress Cataloging in Publication Data
Data available

ISBN 978-0-19-965781-0 (Hbk)
ISBN 978-0-19-870973-2 (Pbk)

CONTENTS

LIST OF FIGURES

LIST OF TABLES

INTRODUCTION

This book began life as the Lyell Lectures in the University of Oxford. I gave them on 3, 5, 10, 12, and 17 May 2011. They were held in the Natural History Museum, a venue which put the textual transmission of the Greek New Testament in perspective by setting it against the backdrop of geological time. I am grateful to the electors for inviting me to give the lectures, and to my audience for its careful engagement and valuable comments and questions.

The lectures had the title 'Describing the New Testament'. I chose it because I wanted to use the word 'describing' in two senses. I began by suggesting that the New Testament has been described, that the role of the scribe and the priority of the manuscript in the formation and development of the works of which it is composed have been denied. As a result, I argued, the New Testament writings have become treated by virtually all readers as though they were a single modern printed work. That is to say, the concept of the modern printed book has become so prevalent that for most users it has driven out other, better informed understandings of the way it came into being and survived. To take a trivial example, readers of English Bibles with subtitles such as 'Paul's work among the Gentiles' are often surprised to be told that they are not an original part of the work, but have been added by a modern editor.[1] But it is not only readers of vernacular translations who make such an assumption. New Testament scholarship taken in the whole pays insufficient attention to the original and subsequent formats and textual transmission of the various works, and treats them together as though they were a printed academic text. The scribe, who was certainly the most important person in keeping writings alive, and to whose skills we owe the survival of anything whatsoever, has been forgotten. But those skills, the opportunities and limitations of writing on a roll or a codex, on papyrus or parchment, in majuscule or minuscule, are the medium through which the works have survived.

Against this, I avowed my desire to 'rescribe the New Testament'. In case you are wondering, there really is a verb 'to rescribe'. You can read all about it in Murray's *New English Dictionary*.[2]

At the same time, I set out to describe the New Testament by describing the documents and the texts out of which the set of works called the New Testament have been made. I argued that there is no other way to describe these works than in the actual forms in which they have been known and are known. I wanted to offer an alternative to the too great influence of the printed text, in favour of the older handwritten medium (which after all survived three times longer than the printed book has so far managed) and the new digital forms which are just beginning to be developed.

When I was revising the lectures for publication, I became dissatisfied with the title, which might seem to be dealing with comparatively superficial matters. I replaced it with the title of this book because I hope that it expresses something more profound, namely that the activities of scribes, typesetters, software developers, and editors do not just tinker with the accidentals and appearance of the New Testament. They have made the New Testament what it is. The New Testament is a collection of books which has come into being as a result of technological developments and the new ideas which both prompted and were inspired by them.

The lectures had the private working title of 'The Beiderbecke Lectures', after Alan Plater's 1985 television series *The Beiderbecke Affair*. I imitated the plays by naming each lecture after its opening words. In fact at one point I was going to take two of Plater's titles by calling the third lecture 'What I don't understand is this...' and the fifth 'We are on the brink of a new era, if only...'. Readers, particularly stemmatologists and digital editors (as well as fans of *The Beiderbecke Affair*), may understand why when they have read the lectures. In the end I decided on more sober titles, though privately I still give them their Beiderbecke names.

The audience which I had in mind, and indeed which attended, consisted largely of bibliographers, editors, and book historians, who are highly expert generically and in their own field, but not necessarily in the realm of New Testament textual scholarship. The book is, I hope, similarly accessible. I have therefore generally introduced manuscripts by their library number and only then used the various numerations of New Testament documents, and tried to avoid taking any subject-specific knowledge for granted. At the same time I trust that the ideas I develop will be of interest to those who are New Testament philologists.

This published form generally follows the spoken text. I have sometimes revised it and occasionally expanded it. The expansion often takes the form of endnotes, a presentation which I generally dislike, but which has proved useful here as a kind of parentheses for filling out points which I had no time to expand in the lecture without interrupting my own flow.

I am grateful to my colleagues at the Institute for Textual Scholarship and Electronic Editing (ITSEE) for being my audience for a trial run of each lecture, and for their many helpful comments and suggestions. It was a particular pleasure to be able to welcome Jim Royse to the run-through of the third lecture and to benefit from his observations.

Bromyard, Herefordshire
December 2011

'THE GENERAL PROCEDURES'

Before I proceed further, I shall beg leave to obviate some miscon-
structions, into which the zeal of some few readers may lead them;
for I would not willingly give offence to any.

Henry Fielding, *The History of Tom Jones, a Foundling*

'The general procedures of textual criticism as it deals with manuscript study have been formulated for some years.' These are not my
words. I begin with a quotation, as perhaps others of those hon-
oured to give these lectures have done, from the fourth person to
give them, the American scholar Fredson Bowers. It is the first sen-
tence of his first lecture, as it appears in printed form in *Bibliography
and Literary Criticism*.[1] Bowers (1905–91) is justly renowned both for
his editions (which included sixteenth- and seventeenth-century
dramatists and a number of later writers) and for his theoretical
work. It is not very surprising to learn that he was also an expert
breeder of dogs. I have always admired his reconstruction of the
composition process of Walt Whitman's *Leaves of Grass*. It was based
upon a study of the types of paper used, the way in which one batch
of poems was written on paper cut out of large sheets, and the cor-
relation of the holes made by the pins which the poet used to attach
the sheets to each other. It seems to me to be as fine a piece of

analysis in the field of bibliography as one could wish to read.[2] These discoveries cast important light on the poems themselves and provided evidence against the claim that Whitman just wrote the stuff without revising it, 'warbling his native woodnotes wild'.

The example of a nineteenth-century poet may seem a strange example with which to begin a discussion of New Testament textual scholarship. It is true that Bowers' work deals with modern printed texts and authorial manuscripts. But there is much for the student of any textual tradition to learn from him. The profundity of his thought and his resourcefulness in finding ways to solve problems (witness the pin holes) are a model that any of us would be proud to emulate. So in beginning my discussions of the New Testament's texts and manuscripts, I choose to begin with Bowers. Let me repeat his words:

The general procedures of textual criticism as it deals with manuscript study have been formulated for some years.

Bowers suggests that the business of critically editing manuscript traditions is all cut and dried because it follows established formulas whereas the textual critic of printed books can no longer work with such confidence. There may here be a hint of the grass on the other side being greener. At any rate, I have to report now that whatever general procedures Bowers could point to in 1959, the world has changed. Were there ever established formulas which were universally applicable? He cites Paul Maas' well-known booklet *Textual Criticism* in support of his view.[3] Maas certainly thought that the right way to edit a text had been established and that if one followed the rules of *recensio* and *examinatio* one could not fail to bring the affair to a successful conclusion. His admirably succinct handbook offers a *vade mecum* to a successful

emendation, recension

6 "go with me" i.e. handbook.

edition. Not many people would be so confident any more, and I am not alone in having always held to the view expressed by Tolstoy in a different connection that every corrupt textual tradition is corrupt in its own way. Each particular situation, which includes the character of the work under consideration, the nature of the manuscripts, and the history of its transmission and reception, has to be treated on its own merits. Certainly, there are principles of logic and common sense and habits of observation and description which every textual scholar has to practise, and I hope that the principles and methodologies addressed in these lectures will be useful in many fields of textual scholarship. But within these principles and methodologies different works and works of different eras require peculiar treatment. Thus, all editors of texts have certain things in common, yet an editor of Homer and an editor of Dante do not carry on their work in the same way.

I suggest therefore that the general procedures of textual criticism as it deals with manuscript study are not so plainly formulated as Bowers supposed.

Moreover, it is worth considering whether we agree with Bowers in the strong contrast he makes between the criticism of manuscripts and the criticism of printed books. In my experience, an editor of Homer will have a certain shared understanding with an editor of James Joyce, even if the differences are more marked than those between editors of manuscript traditions. It seems to me that editors are all in the same boat, for two reasons. First, because we are all dealing with written records, it follows that we are confronted with similar questions concerning the relationship between the origins of a work and its transmitted forms. This is plainest in the discussion of the relationship between an edition and a work's author. We can all applaud when Bowers says that 'we have no means of knowing what ideal form a play took in Shakespeare's mind before he wrote it down', simply substituting gospel or epistle for play and St John or St Paul for Shakespeare.[4] I shall return to this observation, which touches on an essential but little understood aspect of the study of the New Testament, later in this lecture. Secondly, an ancient textual tradition has a 500-year printing history added to it, of which research must take account. Thus, the same process by which Shakespeare's performed plays and Whitman's manuscript poems were printed and published has also moulded the transmission, reception, and interpretation of ancient texts. Editors of the New Testament need to be as alert as the editor of a modern text to the pervasive influence of that printed tradition on the way in which we work.

So, it is doubtful whether the general procedures that Bowers supposed to apply to the study of manuscripts remain applicable. It is also unwise to make too absolute a distinction between the editing of manuscript and printed texts. However, argumentative though I have chosen to be, I do have to concede that there is something in what Bowers says. It is true that editors of ancient manuscript traditions are faced with different situations from editors of works produced in the era of the printed book, that we do not work in exactly the same way, and that we do not use the same terminology. The truth of the first two points is made clear enough when Bowers writes:

The immediate concern of textual bibliography is only to recover as exactly as may be the form of the text directly beneath the printed copy.[5]

The situation of the editor of a text which may be so described is evidently different from that of the editor of the Greek New Testament, who is looking for forms of text more than a thousand years older than the printed copy. The closest analogy to what he is thinking of might be ascertaining which manuscripts Erasmus used in preparing the first printed Greek New Testament in 1516. There is certainly importance in this research, which was of value to the nineteenth-century scholars who replaced Erasmus' with a critical text, but it will be no help at all in our attempt to recover ancient forms of the text.[6]

I take this second quotation from Bowers, with its reference to 'textual bibliography', because it allows me to deal now with questions of terminology. It must be said here and now that the term 'bibliography' in the sense by which this readership is defined is virtually unknown in the field of New Testament textual research. Indeed, almost any practitioner who hears the word will very probably suppose that it means a list of books. This difference in terminology is unfortunate, because it sets a gulf between the study of New Testament texts and manuscripts and other fields of textual research. Why the word should not be used I do not know, but I wonder whether it points to a confusion in New Testament scholarship, since our alternatives to 'bibliography' are not without their problems. What would I prefer to call myself? 'Philologist' I like, though it has the disadvantage that its meaning is better fitted to what I do in its German use than in its narrower English usage.[7] 'Textual critic' I rather dislike, because it does not seem to me very clearly to include the process of editing within it, because it excludes palaeography, and because the word 'critic' can so often encourage the view that we are obsessed with heated debates about minutiae. But it is easily the most common term within the field, and most handbooks contain the phrase within their titles. 'Textologist' I quite like, except for the fact that nobody uses it. 'Textual scholar' and 'textual scholarship' appeal to me, because they are broad terms, and able to include the study of documents as well as the study of texts. I will favour these, with the occasional use of 'bibliography', as paying proper respect to the title of this readership. 'Textual criticism' I will use only with reference to the study of variant readings. I will also refer more explicitly to textual and critical editing as a specific task within the whole field of textual scholarship.

Documents, texts, work

To return to Bowers' opening words: we are now agreed that he was justified in making a distinction between the editing of handwritten and of printed textual traditions. Yet, even so, two questions remain central to all textual scholarship, be it in New Testament research, Shakespeare study, or anything else. The first concerns the relationship between the documents and the text, and the second the relationship between textual and literary criticism. Permit me a little (or you may think considerable) exaggeration, and to say that the materials which we will be discussing are the subject of research by four groups of people.

In the first place we have readers and the many kinds of scholar who are not philologists, who use only a printed edition of the text and completely ignore both the manuscripts and the textual variation lying behind them. Their printed edition may be a critical edition, but it may very well not be. And even if it is, we cannot assume that such a user has considered what the editor's goal has been in establishing a text.

Next come art historians, to whom the written contents function principally as a context for the portraits, embellishments, and decorations which for them are the manuscript's most interesting feature.

Then we meet the textual critics, who are fascinated by every difference between the many versions of the text but pay no attention to the manuscript copies in which they are found, treating them as collections of variant readings and not as physical artefacts, and lose track of the work which the texts represent.

Finally we have the palaeographers, whose concern is in the physical characteristics of the manuscripts, to the extent that they are uninterested in the texts which they contain. In an extreme case they may even neglect to tell us properly what the contents of a manuscript are.

We may describe these interests by three definitions:

- the reader, exegete, and the historian are interested in the *work*, a single form of text distilled from all the varied forms in which it is known;
- the textual critic is interested in the *text*, the form in which the work appears in each manuscript;
- the art historian and the palaeographer are interested in the *document*, the manuscript in which the text is found.

So the exegete will be interested in the Gospel of John, the textual critic in the forms in which the Gospel of John appears in the manuscripts, and the palaeographer in the individual copies of the Gospel of John.[8] This state of affairs is highly unsatisfactory, because no one of the three can be separated from the other two. The work exists as a number of texts, and these texts only exist as documents.

This brings me to an explanation of my title: a scribe who copied some or all of the New Testament books was literally making the (or a) New Testament. An editor who examines the witnesses and from them selects the readings that compose a critical text is also making a New Testament. The team of editors, typesetters, and binders who are responsible for a printed version make a New

Testament. So too do the soft- and hardware experts needed to make a digital New Testament. The New Testament is—and always has been—the result of a fusion of technology of whatever kind is in vogue and its accompanying theory. The theological concept of a canon of authoritative texts comes after. While it is true that we often create the technology that we need rather than stumble upon a technology and then find an application for it, my title seeks to express two truths: that the emergence of the New Testament was not inevitable but a consequence of the activities and experiments of people with a variety of differing skills and interests; and that the New Testament has continued to evolve, so that the New Testament of today is different from the New Testament of the sixteenth century, which in turn is different from that of the ninth. What it will become in the digital age is a fascinating matter to consider. Textual scholarship is more than a descriptive activity. Its practice has been a major influence in the formation and development of the New Testament, both as a concept and as a physical reality.

The title of this work therefore expresses the view that textual scholarship is not an adjunct to the New Testament, or to any other book for that matter. Textual scholarship defines the ways in which we understand a work, even makes its very existence and survival possible. The way in which this works out in the realm of textual editing will become apparent in the third and fourth lectures, and the characteristics of the digital age in the last. More significant than either of these is the importance of the scholars, technicians, and scribes of the ancient world in the evolution of the New Testament. If we are to understand the making of the New Testament, we must try to understand them and their significance. As my original title tried to suggest, the scribe has been forgotten, and as a result we have come to misunderstand what the New Testament is.

Of course, not everyone excludes the scribe from their considera-tion of the New Testament. But it seems to me that the majority do make this mistake, not intentionally but because of the way in which research has developed in the past century. One can see this in the extraordinary fact that most scholars work only with a printed text, and even ignore the critical apparatus which is printed underneath it. Trained though they are to exercise unlimited suspicion with regard to every aspect of the New Testament's historical veracity, question though they do the authorship of many of the works, sceptical though they may be with regard to what can be known about the historical Jesus, adept though they may be at deconstruct-ing the text and reading between the lines, profound though they may be in their interpretations of Pauline theology, they may have the innocence of babes in the way that they trust the printed text. One may even come across a New Testament scholar, as I actually did recently, who, when confronted with a high resolution image of a Greek manuscript of the New Testament had no idea what it was and assumed that it was a badly written modern student exercise.

We need to start in a different place. Let us consider the hierarchy of documents, texts, and work. To understand the *work* we have to understand the *texts* and the *documents*. Take the example of the way in which these lectures will become a book. The process will deter-mine much of the way that I as the author imagine it. I think in typefaces, in hierarchies of punctuation, in sentences and paragraphs, and I have a mental image of how my reader will interpret these physical pointers to the sense.[9] The first-century writer had a com-pletely different set of factors to consider, of which the require-ments of format and of reproduction a copy at a time were not the least. Punctuation was the privilege of the scribe, not the author, and therefore the author needed to convey the work's structure by other means. Such means included a hierarchy of conjunctions and the use of asyndeton, as well as the choice of words to introduce direct speech. There are a lot of things that we do not know about the first Christian writers. But we do possess valuable information about the options that were and were not available to them as writers, or more precisely as authors dictating to an amanuensis. And once we have employed that evidence we will have a better idea concerning what we can and cannot say about them from the historical, exegetical, and theological points of view.

The manuscript tradition

The failure to treat the works in their physical setting and the projection of the anachronism of the printed book onto them—in short, this denial of the tradition as a manuscript tradition transmitted by scribes—is, I suggest, a fundamental methodological error which in turn has been accepted by most other people who are interested in the New Testament. The belief that the printed text is the same thing—either textually or conceptually—as the copies of the first century has had unfortunate results in terms of the study of early Christian history, and of the many uses to which the works are put.[10] From the point of view of bibliography, I point especially to these four problems:

1. The concept of a text dominated by the printed book too easily projects the modern concept of the author onto early Christian writings. I will say more about this in a few moments when I come to discuss the authorial fallacy.

2. Such a concept is also unhelpful when exploring the relationship between oral and written tradition. When authors dictated to

amanuenses, and scribes spoke out loud as they copied, and readers were largely audiences, the distinction cannot have been as absolute as has often been assumed. Perhaps in early Christianity there was simply a tradition, expressed in several media, of which only one survives today. If so, the written part of this tradition may have been less important to early Christians than it is to us. This may be a simple explanation for the fact that the Acts of the Apostles never refers to Paul as a letter writer.

3. The impact on a text of its transmission cannot be appreciated unless we take seriously the difficulties in the ancient world of preserving and disseminating texts. The principal difficulty lay in the fact that each copy had to be made separately. Given the fairly short working life of well-used copies, especially those on papyrus, there was a lot of work involved in keeping the number of documents of a work at a stable level, let alone augmenting it. The uniqueness of each handwritten copy had a further effect. The possibility of having a standard text of a work, which has been a basic assumption to all readers and philologists for five hundred years, was scarcely attainable in the ancient world. We may say that any textual tradition, especially a new one that was unfamiliar to the scribes, was only as good as its worse copyist. Later on, as scribes (and readers) came to know texts intimately, and there were other copies with which to compare anything suspicious, the degree of acceptable variation decreased.) → *i.e. we must attempt to reconstruct and correlate*

Nevertheless, consider the following facts. In a complete collation of the fifteen hundred or so Greek manuscripts containing John 18, there are 1,186 readings which are supported by a minority of manuscripts. This amounts to about thirty in every verse. As many as 555 are found in a single manuscript, 163 have the support of two manuscripts, and 91 are attested by three manuscripts. Only twenty readings have the support of more than one hundred manuscripts. To look at it slightly differently, although there is a clearly attested majority text, consisting of the text of the Byzantine manuscripts, no single manuscript exactly preserves this majority text. Thus, every reader in the Byzantine world will have encountered slight variations. The question we have to consider is the extent to which an awareness of such variations was part of ancient and Byzantine reading. To us the differences between two copies are essential evidence in studying the transmission of a work and the development of its interpretation. But how far were such differences significant to ancient and Byzantine readers, or did they have a mental text which embraced the variation which they encountered? And was this mental text a part of the oral or of the written tradition? Was the meaning which they imparted to the text unaffected by differences which they noticed?

This question is important when one considers the tremendous weight which may be given to precise wording in matters of interpretation. For example, at Romans 5.1 the translations read 'we have peace with God'. But to the printed text's indicative ἔχομεν there is a variant with the subjunctive ἔχωμεν, 'let us have peace'. The cause for the variant is unlikely to be related to the meaning. It is well known that in the Hellenistic period the two words, one with a short and one with a long o, will have been pronounced identically. As a result scribes sometimes wrote down the word more or less regardless of what may have been in their exemplar. They muttered it to themselves, and the sound that came out was more like our way of speaking omega than our way of speaking omicron. We might even have to reckon with the fact that Paul's amanuensis had no way of distinguishing the indicative from the subjunctive. There may be good reasons to judge the short o to be right. But let us not forget that for centuries the hearers of this text were not able to operate with the either/or option which is available to us as users of a printed Greek text, because whatever was written down, what they heard was always more like ἔχωμεν than ἔχομεν. In other words, we may be making a distinction where none was possible, and the better historical interpretation may be one that embraces both possibilities.[11]

We may balance this with another consideration, namely ancient respect for good copies. Augustine plainly did not believe all codices to be equal.[12] And to go further afield, we may see that Galen accorded particular significance to particular codices, perhaps to authorial codices.[13] One might say that even if they knew from experience (just as we do) that perfection in a copy was impossible, some people at least still aspired to as high an accuracy as they could achieve. But we must be pragmatic about the degree of their success.

4. All too often, little attention is paid to the fact that the various works we are considering underwent a process by which they came together into a collection called the New Testament. This process had an effect upon the texts of the individual works. To be sure, in most people's minds the New Testament is a work. But the textual transmission in the manuscript period was almost invariably of single works or collections. Thus, the Gospels and letters were originally in circulation separately in individual rolls. After the adoption of the codex, they were increasingly frequently copied in larger groups, of which the most common is the Gospels, followed by the letters of Paul and then the catholic letters. Occasionally we find a Greek manuscript with all twenty-seven books of the Greek canon. But only with the printed editions of the sixteenth century, made of course in the West under the influence of the Latin tradition, in which the New Testament codex was normal, did the Greek New Testament also become normal.[14]

These four problems illustrate how the projection of the experience of the printed book onto the world of the manuscript can inhibit our attempts to study and to conceptualize the way in which books were conceived, produced, and transmitted in early Christianity.

These four problems may be becoming worse, if I am right in suspecting that one may observe at work a growing conservatism in New Testament scholarship. When Form Criticism was at its most influential in the half-century from the early 1920s onwards, when the work of scholars such as Bultmann, Dibelius, and K. L. Schmidt was widely studied, the Sitz im Leben of the Gospel text was a world of change and uncertainty.[15] Sayings of Jesus were repeated, invented, and remodelled, they were brought into blocks and dispersed again, they were pearls on a string, they were stones polished by use. To the Form Critic there was an oral period, there was a translation from Aramaic to Greek, and there was then a written tradition. But the writing down of the texts did not cause them to become fixed. The heyday of Form Criticism was also an age of new manuscript discoveries, and hence of a steady stream of new readings providing fresh evidence of the changeability of the tradition. Thus the fluid world of the oral tradition was matched by the textual complexity of the documents. But people gradually abandoned this way of studying the tradition, and 'Form Criticism' gave way to 'Redaction Criticism' as a new generation began to read the texts in search of the way in which each writer shaped the tradition. Scholars such as Gunter Bornkamm and Hans Conzelmann proposed theories to describe how an evangelist's redaction of the tradition reveals his distinctive theological views.[16] Such an approach depended upon study of a stable text of each evangelist. In time Redaction Criticism developed into reading each text on its own terms, and finally into a way that included high attention to the reader's response. Where reader response theory dominates, the status of the text itself is taken for granted, since the approach requires a fixed printed text. Reader response theory ignores the critical apparatus, and makes matters worse by identifying the reconstructed critical text as a first-century writer. More than ever before, New Testament scholarship needs to be reminded that 'we have no means of knowing what ideal form a letter took in Paul's mind before he wrote it down', that 'we have no means of knowing what ideal form his Gospel took in Luke's mind before he wrote it down'.

Let us consider what it is to which a reader responds. It is a historically hybrid text: a modern Greek New Testament has been generated from electronic files and printed in its thousands; it has sixteenth-century verse numbers, thirteenth-century chapter numbers, and fourth-century subsections; follows standard rules of orthography partly modern and partly based on manuscripts of the fourth century;[17] has punctuation supplied by its editors; the words are written separately and not in the traditional *scriptio continua*; has the books in the order of the *Latin* Bible; above all the text is based on modern critical study of manuscripts, of which the oldest complete copies were made in the fourth century. The text itself never existed in any ancient document in this precise form (since the individual copy most closely approximating to it will have contained errors that were subsequently corrected), but is a recreation on modern critical principles. It is this mixture of styles and technologies and texts to which readers respond in the belief that they are interacting with the apostle Paul or with the four Gospel writers. Is it not actually the case that they are in debate with the result of two thousand years of development?

To my mind, therefore, bibliography, philology, textual criticism, textual scholarship, call it what you will, has never been so important as it is today. Redressing the situation—*re-scribing* the New Testament—is urgently needed. However, how we do this rescribing is not so simple. It is true that nineteenth- and early twentieth-century scholarship was more aware of the provisional character of the text than people are today. But it is not just a matter of putting the clock back. The old situation also had a serious inbuilt problem. It treated philology, the process of establishing the critical text, as a department of lower criticism, along with grammar and lexicography.[18] Once these foundations had been laid, the construction of the higher criticism of exegesis could proceed all the way up to the chimney pots. But in its own way this approach had as little regard as modern scholarship does for bibliography and philology, because it accepted the premise that the text could be fully and finally established and the textual variation then ignored. However, contemporary textual scholarship has a far higher opinion of itself. Rather than the foundations which are necessary but unseen and ignored, it is the building technique by which you put up the house. It is about finding ways to examine the text which consistently treat it as the kinds of text it has been, rather than as the text which it has become. It constantly reminds everyone concerned with the New Testament that the physical constraints upon authors, copyists, and readers are not accidental factors but substantial considerations which influenced what was written and how the works survived.

The following lectures set out an alternative approach, one which celebrates the scribes and their productions in all their magnificence and drabness, their skill and their limitations, the careful writers and the casual ones, the calligraphy and the scrawls, the workaday and the deluxe. We will attempt to examine the texts and the works of the New Testament with the scribes and the manuscripts always in our minds. In order to achieve this, I propose the following dictum,

That every written work is a process and not an object.

The beguiling format of the book, so evidently a thing we can see, touch, caress, smell, weigh, taste in the case of the seer of the Apocalypse, throw away in disgust, tear in anger, or burn out of fear or hatred, leads to the text and work it represents becoming an object. But this object, the copy, is only a tiny part of the entire process which is the work. At no point can the work in its entirety be defined solely by any one copy. Moreover, our research, of whatever kind it may be, whether it is as exegete, bibliographer, or palaeographer is itself a part of that process. We do not stand above it. In its text and in its format, the work will continue to change, just as it has done throughout its history hitherto. The textual scholarship of each generation and each individual contribution has its value as a step on the road, but is never complete in itself.

This simple and perhaps obvious thought requires a reappraisal of what we think we are doing as textual scholars, and it is this reappraisal which will be the content of my lectures. I shall confine myself to the New Testament, and in fact largely to the Greek New Testament. It is worth mentioning that apart from the thousands of Greek manuscripts there are even more thousands of Latin ones, not to mention copies in Syriac, Coptic, Georgian, Armenian, Ethiopic, Slavic, Gothic, and many other Oriental and Western languages ancient and medieval, many of them with dialectal sub-versions and their own history of recensions. Each of these has its own bibliographical, textual, and cultural history and current significance. It would be impossible to discuss them all. But I hope that what I have to say will be relevant to these other traditions, and indeed to other fields of textual scholarship, just as the contributions of many previous Lyell readers have had an influence beyond their own immediate sphere. I shall address the following topics, each of which will attempt to express a part of the narrative which is textual scholarship.

It will be necessary to take one lecture to discuss the apparently ridiculous question 'What is a New Testament Manuscript?'

In the third lecture I shall address ways of understanding how manuscripts are related, by assessing the history of New Testament textual scholarship and describing the new approaches which we are developing in Birmingham and Münster.

The fourth lecture will deal with critical editions. I will discuss their purpose and character, and describe the procedures we are developing today in making the largest ever critical edition of the New Testament.

In the fifth lecture I will discuss how our research is changing, how it may change in the immediate future and what the New Testament of the future may be like. In short, I will give you my textual Utopia, before bringing the series to a conclusion.

In order to set the scene for these discussions, I will devote the rest of this lecture to introducing a number of important questions which must be considered.

Textual and manuscript studies

Returning to my prime text for the day, I take up in another way Bowers' view that 'The general procedures of textual criticism as it deals with manuscript study have been formulated for some years.' I wish now to consider how we imagine the relationship between textual criticism and manuscript study, between texts and documents. In fact, we have to ask a number of fundamental questions about the relationship between the two. We will discuss the right understanding of the differing significance of a document and of *we must give an account for the word, before interpreting the word.*

the text contained in a document in the third lecture. Here I offer
only the general observation that it seems to be the case that manuscript studies exist in their own right, by virtue of the fact that the
manuscripts exist. Textual criticism, on the other hand, is dependent
on manuscript studies and needs to find a way of describing how
the individual forms of a text in the manuscripts may be synthesized
as a single work. And yet the comparison of the forms of text which
they contain is an important aspect of the study of the manuscripts.
Can we therefore say that textual criticism is simply a part of the
study of manuscripts? I consider that to be accurate in principle and
theoretically. A document without a text can exist (see the Chester
Beatty papyrus discussed in Lecture 2). But a text cannot exist without a document.

At any rate, nobody forces anyone to make critical editions or to
analyse the many forms in which texts exist. We could simply get by
using manuscripts, or at any rate surrogates of manuscripts. But for
all sorts of reasons this is not very practicable. Manuscripts are not
necessarily accessible, they require editing to be intelligible to most
users, and it is certainly very convenient in discussing a work if we
are all using a copy with similar wording. As a result, we exist in a
real world where critical editions—and sometimes very uncritical
ones—are all around us and are the mode in which we share our
views about written works. Historically, it is the textual research
which has driven manuscript studies.[19]

Texts in early Christianity

We have now to consider another question which is of the utmost
importance, namely the concept of the critical text. I return to the
quotations from Bowers, that 'The immediate concern of textual

bibliography is only to recover as exactly as may be the form of the text directly beneath the printed copy' and that 'we have no means of knowing what ideal form a play took in Shakespeare's mind before he wrote it down'. The view that there is one form of text to be recovered is not self-evident but a matter that needs to be considered. I have argued consistently that this is not necessarily true.[20] With regard to the Gospels, for example, I have suggested that in the earliest period of their transmission the individuals and communities who read them and passed them on considered themselves free to adapt the wording, the letter, to bring out the meaning, the spirit. The evangelists themselves, who evidently felt comfortable about adapting the tradition quite substantially, cannot but have reckoned with their own work being similarly treated in due course. The evidence I presented for this view was substantially the existence of the many variant readings which alter the sense of the Gospels, especially of the words of Jesus. In the context of this actual situation in early Christianity, I argued, the modern concept of a single authoritative 'original' text was a hopeless anachronism, foisting on early Christianity something that can only exist as a result of modern concepts of textual production. Instead, I suggested that the variety of the oldest forms of the text should be acknowledged and made an integral part of the way in which the work is read or studied. The degree of variation which we find in the Gospels is the most obvious example of the textual freedom which, I argued, may be seen in early Christianity. But it appears elsewhere too. To take some obvious examples, there is the paraphrastic version of Acts already known from Codex Bezae and now attested in another form in a recently published Oxyrhynchus papyrus; and there is the fact that Romans also existed in at least one shorter form.[21]

If early Christians were prepared to change the text in order to bring out what they believed to be its true meaning, what are we doing if we try to exchange that pluriformity for a single critical text? Should we not be embracing the multiformity of the text? This is an important question with regard to the nature of a critical edition, which I will return to in the fourth lecture. For the moment, let me simply say that a critical edition is much more than a critical text.

This brings me to my next topic.

The critical text

In each of the New Testament writings, the philologist's task is to recover the form of text from which the surviving copies are descended. The most important thing to be said at this stage is that such a form of text is not the same thing as an original or authorial text. This reconstruction is called the Ausgangstext or Initial Text in the methodology of Münster and Birmingham. Let me say at once that there is nothing new in this distinction. The concept of an oldest recoverable text is certainly as old as Richard Bentley, who wrote in 1716 that

I find I am able (what some thought impossible) to give an edition of the Gr. Test. exactly as it was in the best examples at the time of the Council of Nice.[22]

Thus Bentley understood that it was possible to go so far back on the basis of a comparison of the extant witnesses, but no further. Certainly, the year 325 is a striking improvement on the received text deriving from Erasmus and based on Byzantine copies which Bentley wished to replace with his own edition. Today we are able to improve on Bentley for some parts of some writings, since we have a few copies which even give us evidence about some of the forms in which several works existed in the third century. But there still remains a gap between the form of text from which we conclude by critical examination that the extant witnesses must be descended and the yet older form or forms from which that oldest recoverable text must be descended.

Understanding this gap and recognizing the limitations of the critical edition is of the utmost importance for all users. With regard to present purposes, it allows me to rephrase Bowers' statement to fit the situation of New Testament scholarship to read as follows:

The immediate concern of textual bibliography is only to recover as exactly as may be the oldest recoverable forms of the text beneath the manuscript copies.

Recognizing that there is a gap between the oldest recoverable forms of the text and the creation of the work requires us to address one final topic.

The authorial fallacy

To repeat, 'we have no means of knowing what ideal form a letter took in Paul's mind before he wrote it down' and 'we have no means of knowing what ideal form his Gospel took in Luke's mind before he wrote it down'. We can underline emphatically that the authorial fallacy *is* a fallacy. The New Testament philologist's task is *not* to recover an original authorial text, not only because we cannot at present know on philological grounds what that original text might have been, nor even because there may have been several forms to the tradition, but because philology is not able to make a pronouncement as to whether or not there was such an authorial text. The best it can do with regard to the New Testament is to use evidence derived from our study of the extant tradition to present a model of the problems with the concept of the author. This will include the character of a manuscript tradition in antiquity (see page 15 above) and the development of suggestions (such as those offered in my *Living Text of the Gospels*) that attempt to argue on the basis of the hard evidence of textual variation.

The relationship between the Initial Text and whatever went before it is naturally a very interesting matter, not least because it seems to me that the role of bibliography becomes completely different in such an inquiry. We would be using the manuscripts in two ways. First, as bearers of the readings and kinds of readings which existed in the period predating the Initial Text. Secondly, as evidence (or perhaps a model) for understanding the physical forms in which the works had been transmitted in the period before the writing of the oldest surviving manuscript. In the case of the New Testament, this is especially important, for an important change in the format of the copies occurred between the formation of the writings and the copying of the oldest surviving manuscripts. This was the transition in their format from scroll to codex. What we know about the possibilities and limitations of each format, and the differences between them, can go some way towards establishing a working model of the way in which the text may have developed. For example, where a number of texts such as the Gospels or the Pauline letters are too long to have fitted onto a roll, we may develop theories about the way in which the individual works may have circulated as rolls and how the adoption of the codex form made it possible to make them part of a larger unit.

As I have said, the task of editing is to reconstruct the oldest available form of a work by analysis of the texts that appear in the extant witnesses. This is a logical process which unveils the history of the text and its oldest form. It cannot itself have anything to say about the relationship of that oldest form to an authorial text. For example, the oldest form of the Gospel of John recoverable by textual criticism undoubtedly has Chapter 6 after Chapter 5 and finishes with Chapter 21. Any questions regarding the possibility that the authorial text (even supposing that there was such a thing) might have had Chapter 6 *before* Chapter 5 and lacked Chapter 21 is not the textual critic's but somebody else's business. The Pericope Adulterae, on the other hand, is very much a topic for textual criticism, because the study of the manuscripts reveals that some contain it and some do not; this observation requires an explanation and an editorial decision, whether to exclude it or to include it.

It has to be emphasized that most of what I have just outlined is disputed in some way or other. Not everyone believes in my theory of the emergence of the Gospel text. Not everyone has got to grips with the theory of the Initial Text. There are many aspects of the history of the early Christian book which are not understood or are currently interpreted in more than one way. It is even more telling that there is little general understanding or discussion of the nature, purpose, and status of a critical edition. In my judgement this is a very important matter to consider in revisiting the relationship between bibliography and textual criticism. As the person who came up with a theory of the living text of the Gospels and as one of the tiny number of people employed in making a critical edition of the New Testament, I am probably uniquely qualified to appreciate the niceties of the situation.[23] I have had to ask myself whether I am trying to maintain a tension between two irreconcilable opinions, and my answer is that I do believe that it is possible to reconstruct an Initial Text and to hold my view of the texts' earlier history. We can use philology to reconstruct an Initial Text. But we need not then believe that the Initial Text is an authorial text, or a definitive text, or the only form in which the works once circulated. It is also possible that we may reach the conclusion that our extant manuscripts are descended not from one single Initial Text, but from several. In fact I believe that once we achieve as full as possible a reconstruction of the history of the text we will be in a better position than we have ever been before to study the period predating the Initial Text.

Documents, texts, works

The hierarchy of documents, texts, works will be an important part of my presentation. It is in fact remarkable how often we use the word 'text' loosely. To reiterate: a work is, for example, the Gospel of John. A document is a writing containing that work, for example, Codex Sinaiticus. A text is the form of the work contained in that manuscript. This hierarchy is the ontology developed for the Virtual Manuscript Room (http://www.vmr.bham.ac.uk/) built in Birmingham to search for and gather relevant materials. It was funded by the Joint Information Systems Committee (JISC) programme 'Exposing digital content for reuse (jiscEXPO)'.[24] Here is an example of the rigour demanded by a computer programme requiring us to think more carefully about our discipline as a whole. Distinguishing between these three entities will have important implications for research, as well as providing a way of linking analogous data.

Conclusion

I have not used any visual aids in this lecture. This is a little perverse, since the digital medium is transforming bibliography. In the following lectures I will frequently use examples of the products of mass digitization, the hundreds of images which are going online every day.[25] Never before have philologists been so closely in touch with the primary data of their research, and this is especially true of those branches of research pertaining to ancient texts. Not only do we have access to high resolution images of copies preserved for centuries in libraries, we can also now look at ones which until the last few decades had spent fifteen hundred years and more underground, in rubbish heaps and hiding places and wherever they were abandoned. Moreover, we are developing powerful tools for recording and analysing complex information about the images and the text we may read in them, as later lectures will show. For today's themes, it is enough to observe that the advent of the digital text has allowed us to see the era of the printed text as what may prove a short intermission in the much longer history of the book, and has given us new categories for the ways in which we imagine ancient manuscript traditions.

I should add a word of warning, that in the case of biblical research bibliography will inevitably find theology dragged into it at some point. Where a text is revered by some people as divinely inspired, in some cases as a verbally precise pronouncement by an all-powerful God, or even at its least dramatic when it is viewed as a helpful guide for daily life, the findings of the bibliographer may be of particular importance.

And in case we get too carried away with the importance of penmanship and of the texts by which it is preserved, let us remember that our codices are not all in all, and may be no more than a by-product of our lives. As Katherine Swift has put it in her book *The Morville Hours*:

It was the acorns that made the oak so important to country-dwellers. Not for them the oak's hard wood, destined for the timbers of great ships or the roofs of lofty halls. Nor the bark used in the stinking vats of the leather tanner. Nor yet the oak galls, used for making ink. Pigs were what mattered to the peasants, and acorns were what mattered to pigs.[26]

I take this as a reminder of two things: that texts are only a part of human affairs and discourse, and that while you can eat without being a textual critic, the reverse is not possible.[27]

WHAT IS A NEW TESTAMENT MANUSCRIPT?

What a place to be in is an old library! It seems as though all the souls of all the writers, that have bequeathed their labours to these Bodleians, were reposing here, as in some dormitory, or middle state.

Charles Lamb, 'Oxford in the Vacation'

What is a New Testament manuscript? The question is rarely asked, but when we begin to do so, we will quickly encounter a number of difficulties of definition which run through the centuries and call into question the boundaries that have been drawn. I have already developed the theme that in order to understand a work we need to understand the documents and the texts in which that work is found. Before going on I should add that in the field of Greek New Testament bibliography there are generally said to be three classes of witnesses to each work:

Greek manuscripts
citations of the work found in works by early Christian writers
translations, themselves consisting of manuscripts and citations.

In this lecture I will mainly discuss Greek manuscripts. But citations and versions will also be mentioned.

First, some basic facts and figures:

How many 'New Testament manuscripts' are there? This is a moving figure, but the answer as of early May 2011 was:

Papyri	125
Majuscules	284
Minuscules	2,820
Lectionaries	2,377

This gives a total of 5,606.[1]

The papyri date between the second and eighth centuries, the majuscules between the third and eleventh centuries, and the minuscules between the ninth and nineteenth centuries.[2] The lectionaries date almost wholly between the eighth and nineteenth centuries (see Figure 2.1).[3]

The ability to offer an exact number (even though it is illusory) indicates that there is an authoritative source. The universally accepted list of manuscripts is produced by the Münster Institute for New Testament Textual Research, and is known by its shortest possible title, the German word *Liste*. The *Liste*, now in its second edition, gives a one-line entry for each manuscript.

The information given reveals the work's purpose. There is sufficient summary information (1) to identify a manuscript and (2) to abstract a list of all manuscripts in the *Liste* containing a particular

Figure 2.1: Distribution of manuscripts by century

work or works. One could also, with a little trouble, find all manuscripts written in the thirteenth century, or all manuscripts with twenty-three lines to a page. But it is clearly designed primarily to provide the basic information about all the copies of a work. That work is the collection of works called the New Testament. Thus, the *Liste* is designed as the basic requirement for a critical edition, namely a complete list of the potential witnesses to be included. The link with the critical edition is demonstrated also by its origins, which can be found in a survey by C. R. Gregory published in 1908, which is itself a development of the same scholar's lists of manuscripts accompanying Tischendorf's eighth edition, published in 1884.[4]

Before going any further, let us look again at the *Liste*'s four categories of manuscript: papyri, majuscules, minuscules, and lectionaries. Until just over a century ago, there were three, and all known extant copies were written on either parchment or paper: majuscules (all on parchment), minuscules, and lectionaries (these two groups on parchment, paper, or a mixture of the two). The first two categories broadly divide continuous-text manuscripts into two groups on the basis of their script, older ones (majuscules) and newer ones (minuscules).

Lectionaries are an undifferentiated class, containing the readings in the order in which they were read. By the time that copies written on a third material, papyrus, began to be discovered, these three classes were already extensive, and it probably seemed obvious to introduce a fourth class containing this category of manuscript. There is no other justification (although the oldest papyri predate the oldest majuscules, the first ones to be discovered were coeval with them), and in terms of logic it adds a confusing third criterion for classification, that of material. We may already see that the business of listing the extant copies cannot be altogether straightforward.

We begin to find some further underlying problems when we consider the categories in more detail.

The papyri

I begin with the manuscripts of the early centuries written on papyrus. What does a manuscript have to do to qualify? First and obviously, it has to have been written on papyrus, *Cyperus papyrus*. And all our examples do indeed meet this criterion. Secondly, it must contain some part of the New Testament in Greek. But it is here that the system breaks down. It is true that all the papyri listed in Münster do indeed contain some New Testament text in Greek. But there are a number of other papyri which also contain New Testament text in Greek but are excluded from this 'official' list.

Papyri are often pretty scrappy remains, and it can be difficult to work out what a manuscript once was on the basis of as little as a single fragment of a single leaf. In particular, we cannot always know whether it is the remains of a manuscript which once contained an entire work or set of works, or was always a single sheet which may have been used for some purpose which did not necessarily include reading. Thus a papyrus from the Ashmolean, containing parts of four verses from Jude, may be the remains of an amulet.[5] It is included in the *Liste*, and cited in critical editions. But another text, which is also an amulet to judge by the way it was once folded up and by the magical symbols which it contains in the upper margin, containing the first two verses each of Psalm 90, Romans 12, and John 2, is not included in the list and therefore does not feature in editions.[6] There are other documents which combine a mixture of biblical and non-biblical text, such as several manuscripts with sentences for fortune-telling written below the biblical text.[7]

Where there is only a scrap surviving, we do not know whether it is from an amulet, a continuous-text or lectionary manuscript, or even a homily or a commentary. At the most extreme, we might even have to say that there are no absolute grounds for determining whether a Gospel fragment is a copy of a canonical or a non-canonical Gospel. Without going into endless examples, there are inconsistencies between the inclusion and exclusion of papyrus fragments, whether on grounds of

purpose (text or amulet)
contents (biblical and non-biblical)
function (homily with biblical text, lectionary, non-canonical Gospel).[8]

These difficulties of classification have significant implications, in particular with regard to the canon. Often in the examples I have been discussing the amount of text is very slight. The problem is more dramatically highlighted when we consider Papyrus Bodmer VII, VIII, and IX, the Bodmer Miscellaneous Codex, a compilation containing the work of four scribes made over the course of some years. It contains eleven works:

the Nativity of Mary, also known as the *Protevangelium Iacobi*
3 Corinthians
the eleventh Ode of Solomon
the letter of Jude
Melito of Sardis' *Homily on the Passion* (late second century)
a fragment from a hymn
The Apology of Phileas, written in the beginning of the fourth century
Psalms 33.2–34.16
the letters of Peter.

A number of important and probably unanswerable questions remain concerning the composition and sequence of this collection.

For the moment, let us just note that this codex has the right to be included in catalogues of manuscripts of the Septuagint, the New Testament, and several other writings, as well as preserving one otherwise unknown text (the hymn).[9] So while the letters of Peter and Jude may be canonical now, and may have been on the road to canonical status at the period during which the papyrus was produced (it is one of the two oldest copies of these works), the document itself is what it is: a compilation. As editors and students of the New Testament, we may consider ourselves entitled to pick out the texts that interest us. After all, the editor of the *Protevangelium* will pick out just that work from the collection. But even if one does so, it is important to remember that the text of the letters of Peter and of Jude which it contains exist as a part of this unique collection. It has been argued by Nicklas and Wasserman that the codex had a liturgical environment and that this environment influenced the wording of the text of Jude.[10] It appears that the nature of the manuscript as a compilation is essential evidence for the textual critic. Thus the presence of a part of this document in the *Liste* as a 'New Testament manuscript' will be misleading if the text it contains is divorced from that context.

We may apply the question of the canon in discussing the other documents we have mentioned. The magical text with part of John and the amulet of Jude may contain sentences from canonical works, but as documents it is hard to see how one could describe them as canonical. This distinction is an important one, and I shall return to it later. Meanwhile, it is worth holding it in the back of our minds as we consider other categories of manuscript.

Before coming to that, I will refer to one other unexpected category of papyrus in the *Liste*. P99 (Chester Beatty Ac. 1499, fols 11–14) is a Graeco-Latin glossary of selected lemmata from Romans,

2 Corinthians, Galatians, and Ephesians. The manuscript also contains paradigms, juridical glosses, and a majority of blank leaves.
From one perspective this inclusion seems very strange. What may
have led to its inclusion is its textual interest: the Greek and the
Latin texts are both distinctive.[11]

Parchment majuscule manuscripts, amulets, ostraca, and inscriptions

The questions of canonicity which we met in looking at the
Bodmer Miscellaneous Codex recur in the same way with some of
our oldest parchment codices: both Codex Sinaiticus and Codex
Alexandrinus contain early Christian texts which are not canonical,
as well as the larger Greek canon of the Septuagint.[12] Codex
Sinaiticus contains the Epistle of Barnabas and the Shepherd of
Hermas, and Codex Alexandrinus contains 1 and 2 Clement. We
may say that these are one-volume copies of essential Christian reading, which happen to include all the books of the Western canon. Is
the problem formally any different from that with the Bodmer
Miscellaneous Codex? Is the difference simply in the fact that these
parchment codices contain a majority of canonical works, so that the
problem is masked, while with the papyrus it is the non-canonical
works that are in the majority? In both, the concept of canonicity is
linked to individual works, not to the document as a whole.

As with the papyri, many of the more recently discovered majuscule manuscripts consist only of one or a few leaves, so we cannot
comment on their original contents.

In several ways the list of majuscules in the *Liste* is at least as
problematical as the list of papyri. Two fragmentary manuscripts
contain sentences for fortune-telling. The only difference between

them and the examples on papyrus is the material used.[13] One entry is a small fragment from a roll containing a Gospel Harmony, and is therefore not a work to be found in the New Testament.[14] Two more are even stranger: one (0152) refers to talismans, which is simply another word for amulets. This sequence was inaugurated by von Dobschütz, and extended to nine items in 1933, after which it fell from use.[15] The second entry (0153) lists ostraca. It extended to twenty-five items before it too was abandoned. It is clearly strange to include shards of pottery in a list of parchment manuscripts. Can a New Testament manuscript be a few words on a potsherd? Whatever answer there may be to the question, we must not ignore these witnesses. One Coptic ostracon contains the story of the woman taken in adultery in Sahidic, which passage is absent in the Sahidic manuscripts of the Gospel of John. The ostracon is therefore the only witness to the text of the passage in this version.[16] When the entry 0153 was originally devised by C. R. Gregory in the early years of the twentieth century, it consisted only of a single collection of twenty ostraca. This set, which remains the most extensive, was found by Bouriant in Upper Egypt in the late nineteenth century and published by Lefebvre in 1905. They have been dated to the fifth or sixth century.[17] The longest section is Luke 22.40–70.[18] The extract even goes to the trouble to tell us what Gospel it is from. I have not yet managed to locate any images of them. But the drawing in the edition allows one to reconstruct the shape. One might say that if parchment manuscripts are the word made flesh, these are the word made clay. The choice of old pots for a writing material is based on the availability of other alternatives. Sometimes texts on them may be extensive, such as a school exercise extending to 250 lines.[19] It does not in itself imply that the copy is intended to have a lower status. From the editorial point of view, we have therefore to take these copies as seriously as any other in the process of assessing the evidence and reconstructing a critical text.

The *Liste* has never included another rarely considered category of evidence, lapidary inscriptions. I do not want to say very much about inscriptions, except to observe that we have little up-to-date information about them. Their total exclusion does seem arbitrary. An example of an inscription of some interest is found on Absalon's Pillar. It contains Luke 2.25 with a form of one word similar to that found in Codex Sinaiticus.[20]

Thus the class of majuscules is not without its problems either. When we turn to the minuscules, we again find something unexpected.

The minuscules

Because they are the most numerous category, because many of them are late in date, and because the majority of them are much more uniform textually than the oldest copies, the minuscules have received comparatively little attention from New Testament scholars. On the other hand, to historians of Byzantine art, illuminated copies are naturally of great interest, and I will discuss the value of this approach in the next lecture. It may be that there are other problems which I have not considered, but here I will focus on a single one.[21]

Commentary manuscripts

I said at the beginning that there are 2,820 minuscule manuscripts. Within them we find two classes. The first consists of those which, for the most part, contain biblical text. There may be prefaces or occasional marginal notes, canon tables, or chapter lists. But the vast amount of the text comprises a part (very rarely even all) of the New Testament. Gospel manuscripts are the most common, followed by Praxapostoloi, of which some contain only Paul's letters, with copies of the Apocalypse running a clear fourth.

What is surprising is the discovery that there are also a considerable number which contain an extensive commentary as well as a New Testament text. At this point a brief history of the commentary is in order to explain the situation.

Let us consider the choices open in different epochs to scholars wishing to write about or to edit texts. The simplest has always been the annotation, the gloss. It consists of an interlinear or marginal note, sometimes so similar in appearance to the text on which it comments that the suggestion that they were sometimes mistaken by subsequent users as part of the text is very reasonable. But the annotator suffered from the restriction of space, since the extent of unwritten area available had been laid down by the scribe of the manuscript, who was concerned only with the existing text. We sometimes see scribes themselves suffering from this problem, where they have made some mistake of omission and are hard-pressed to fit in the missing text. So the opportunity for written comment on the text was generally restricted to altering the wording. Much later, in the medieval West, large-format manuscripts would be produced which contained the biblical text, the gloss, and ample space for users to add their own notes. But in early Christianity, this problem was resolved with the adoption (most notably by Origen) of the commentary. In fact the rather limited amount of text one could get even onto a papyrus codex, let alone a roll, meant that someone with as much to say as Origen had needed the freedom of a limitless number of rolls. This meant that the annotations could be kept separate from the text under observation, and could be as long as the commentator chose. The opportunity to commentate may have been at least partly responsible for the text's increasing stability, since alternative renderings were no longer necessary. At this point, it seems reasonable to say that two types of work existed independently: the one is found in manuscripts containing the biblical text, the other in manuscripts containing a commentary. Thus it seems fairly simple to distinguish between a copy of the Gospel of John and a copy of Origen's commentary upon it. The first may be described as a New Testament manuscript, and the second may not. But all commentary manuscripts are to some extent witnesses to the text of the Gospel of John through the forms of text either contained in them or implied by the commentator's observations. Some commentators liked to include the whole text of a block of text to be discussed, so that the entire biblical work is present as headings to the commentary. (The work will also be at least partially present as running text in the body of the commentary, in forms which may differ in wording from the lemmata.) Some gave only a part of that text as a guide to what was coming, so that the biblical text is incomplete. All such pieces of text will be classed as patristic citations of the Gospel of John (see pages 32 above and 116–17 below).[22]

Such is the commentary by a single author. A few centuries later, someone devised the catena. This consists of a series of excerpts from different commentaries, brought back onto the same page as the biblical text. The catena became possible because of the much greater amount of text that could be written into a parchment codex. This type of gloss went through several formats. In what seems to be the oldest the sacred text was kept in its own text block, surrounded on three sides by the catena. Not only that, but the scribe could use two different scripts, one for the biblical text and one for the commentary. We may see it in the oldest such manuscript extant, Codex Zacynthius.[23] We can see similar conventions also over three hundred years later in a manuscript which uses two forms of minuscule.[24]

The more common format had a single text block with the biblical text as a series of lemmata preceding the comment upon it, in the same layout in fact as the commentary. There are two principal layouts for this format. In the first, biblical text is written on separate lines from the commentary. The Codex Monacensis 30 is such a manuscript, which has been dubiously classed as a majuscule.[25] There is a majuscule hand in use for the biblical text and a minuscule one for the commentary, in alternating blocks of text. The biblical text is clearly marked even in manuscripts written wholly in minuscule.[26] In the second layout, the biblical text is found fully embedded in the commentary text.[27] Here it can be somewhat harder to locate. In both formats, its distinctiveness could be marked by a different script, by the use of red ink, or by the placing of markers in the margin against the lines of biblical text. Sometimes such systems broke down through a scribe's confusion or forgetfulness, and one must seek for the biblical text among the masses of commentary. These can be the hardest manuscripts to read and understand, much like Merlin's book in *The Idylls of the King*:

> The text no larger than the limbs of fleas;
> And every square of text an awful charm,
> Writ in a language that has long gone by.
> And every margin scribbled, crost and cramm'd
> With comment, densest condensation, hard

> To mind and eye
> And none can read the text, not even I.[28]

There are a considerable number of such manuscripts. For example, out of nearly two thousand copies with a Gregory-Aland number containing the Gospel of John, about 250 are catena manuscripts. At least one hundred of them contain the compilation by Theophylact (1055–1107). Another named catenist is Nicetas, archbishop of Heraclea where the Lycus flows into the Black Sea, whose catena of the Gospel of John was written in about 1080. A third is Euthymius Zigabenus, who compiled his work around the year 1100. Johannes Reuss unearthed a labyrinth of anonymous types A and B and C with basic forms and expansions and abridgements and unique manuscripts.[29] Each type has its own blend of passages. The tradition, from Codex Zacynthius onwards, is to name the excerpted writer in the margin. John Chrysostom is always the most popular.[30]

We now have three kinds of manuscripts, if we follow the standard classification:

- those containing texts of the work *The Gospel of John*;
- those containing texts of a work that is a commentary;
- and those containing texts of a work that is a fusion of a number of commentaries.

It seems reasonable to conclude that the first category may reasonably be listed as manuscripts of the New Testament, and that the second are not copies of the New Testament, even though they may contain the complete biblical work in the form of lemmata. Before I go on I need to draw your attention to another inconsistency in the list of New Testament manuscripts. A number of manuscripts have been included in the *Liste* which are commentaries and not catenae. For example, five manuscripts are copies of Cyril of Alexandria's Commentary on John.[31] According to the criteria, these should be bracketed, along with manuscripts already bracketed, such as Vaticanus Palatinus graecus 32 (Gregory-Aland 882), which is already noted as being a copy of Chrysostom's Homilies on John.

But what about the third category? These texts are witnesses to three different works: the biblical book contained in lemmata and running texts; the work composed by the excerptor who made the catena; and the works to which those excerpts originally belong. In fact, since some catena types are revisions of existing catenae, the texts of a later type are also witnesses to as many older catena forms as it was derived from.

Are such catena manuscripts to be described as New Testament manuscripts or not? It is reasonable to argue that they are not, that like the manuscripts of works such as Origen's commentaries, they have no place in a list of manuscripts of the New Testament, and therefore must not be cited among the continuous-text witnesses along with P75, Codex Vaticanus, and the rest. Given the way in which the commentary tradition moves very slowly, with one writer modifying and building on predecessors, one might argue that formally every commentary has at least a whiff of the catena about it (and if you compare a dozen modern commentaries on a work, you will see that I am not necessarily talking about the ancient world). Thus, a catena may be described as a particular form of Byzantine commentary, not as a separate genre requiring special treatment. It is possible that one might be justified in treating those like Codex Zacynthius with a separate text block differently from those with the lemmata divided between sections of comment, since these at least have the biblical work in a continuous whole. But it is not clear that this difference in format indicates any difference in genre of the work, purpose of the copy or status of the biblical text.

At this point, though, we are reaching the conclusion that it has been a mistake to include the catena manuscripts, certainly those of the second and third format which I described.

However, there turn out to be surprisingly good reasons why we have to pay careful attention to this kind of manuscript. I will discuss these reasons shortly. But first I must point out a glaring anomaly in the system, which suggests that New Testament textual scholars have not been certain about the status of the catena manuscripts. It came as a great surprise to me to find that there are many catena manuscripts which are not counted as New Testament witnesses by being given a Gregory-Aland number, even though they are of the same type as manuscripts which are included and have the same format. At the most extreme, Reuss listed twenty-two manuscripts of John containing what he calls the basic form of Type A. Of these, only five have been given a Gregory-Aland number. There are therefore seventeen manuscripts of the same catena and with the same general appearance which have been excluded. To take another example, Reuss lists one manuscript (Codex Vaticanus graecus 1610) of the Catena of Makarios Chrysokephalos (who I believe to have lived in the fourteenth century). It is not in the *Liste*. So we have here a particular catena which is not represented at all.

Moreover, if we look at Reuss' index of manuscripts, we will see that he must have searched only a few library catalogues—apart from one Mar Saba manuscript his references are all to manuscripts in notable Western collections (of which just one is in the United Kingdom).[32] One may speculate that the true number of catena manuscripts lacking from the *Liste* may even be as many as those that have been included.

We find therefore that there are two serious problems with this rather numerous category of catena manuscript: that many have not been included among the New Testament manuscripts and that arguably none of them should have been included.

So would it be best to excise the catena manuscripts from the reckoning, and count only the minuscule manuscripts containing the biblical text? This would appear to be consistent, and would solve the problem of the list being so deficient. But there are strong reasons why this is the less satisfactory solution. The most remarkable thing is that some of these catena manuscripts contain a very interesting and influential text. I take the example of a manuscript containing a catena on John written around the year 1000, Rome, Biblioteca Vallicelliana E.40 (Gregory-Aland 397). According to Reuss, it is the only manuscript (which he found) of a particular class, which he called Type D.[33] If we look at the Gospel text of this manuscript in the data collected from 153 test passages in John 1–10, we find that it has a very low percentage of agreement with the majority Byzantine text, namely 61.4 per cent.[34] Of a total of 1,763 manuscripts that were examined, only twenty-six manuscripts have a lower percentage of agreement with the Majority Text, and of those twelve are extant in so few test passages (five or fewer) that the statistics have no validity (see Table 2.1).

If you turn it round and start with the texts agreeing most closely with the provisional oldest form of text currently available, that in the Nestle-Aland *Novum Testamentum Graece*, it comes thirteenth (see Table 2.2).[35]

If one takes the two tables together, they contain nineteen manuscripts (nine feature in both of them): P45 P66 P75 01 03 04 05 019 029 032 032S 033 050 070 083 086 317 397 849. Of these, five are commentary manuscripts: 033 050 317 397 849.

Table 2.1: Manuscripts extant in at least ten test passages having fewer agreements with the Majority Text than does 397

397	61.4%
033	61.2%
317	57.1%
019	48.4%
849	46.7%
P66	44.8%
032S	44%
04	41.7%
05	41.3%
01	36.7%
032	36.3%
03	34.6%
029	34.1%
P75	33.8%
P45	14.3%

Another indicator of a significant text is the list of Sonderlesarten, readings which are neither shared by the majority of manuscripts nor adopted in the Nestle-Aland edition. In this list 397 comes thirty-fourth with twenty-four readings.[36] The significance of this may be gauged by the fact that this is about the same number as some of the leading members of Family 1, a significant family of Gospel manuscripts whose oldest extant members date to the ninth century and whose text is an important witness. One would therefore be hard put to justify ignoring this manuscript, which stands fifteenth in a list of manuscripts disagreeing most with the Byzantine mainstream

Table 2.2: Manuscripts extant in at least ten test passages agreeing more closely than 397 with Nestle-Aland 27

050	90%
029	84.1%
086	83.3%
03	80.4%
P75	78.4%
083	77.8%
04	76.7%
019	73.9%
032	70.6%
849	66.7%
070	65.5%
032S	62%
397	60.1%

and thus regularly agreeing with some of the oldest manuscripts of John, both in good and in poor readings.

The picture becomes a little richer when we look for manuscripts closely related to Gregory-Aland 397 in the same 153 test passages, using the grouping tools devised by the Münster Institute.[37] These are the manuscripts which agree with 397 more often than 397 agrees with the Majority Text:[38]

865 (73.15 per cent agreement with 397 in the test passages)
033 (72.94 per cent)
33 (71.71 per cent)
019 (71.24 per cent).

Of these four manuscripts, two have a catena and two do not. The two catena manuscripts (865 and 033) belong, according to Reuss, in his Group A. 865 is a late manuscript, not older than the fifteenth century.[39] 033 is of the tenth century, and so close in date to 397. The two without a catena are 019 (eighth century) and 33 (ninth century). Thus 397's closest links are with manuscripts both within and beyond the catena tradition, and with them it represents a very old form of the text. Although it has very few relations and none that are very close, it has only one singular reading in the test passages and there are very few of its Sonderlesarten in which it does not agree with one or more of the most significant papyri and fourth- and fifth-century majuscules.

That a catena manuscript should have so striking a text is not as surprising to us today as it might once have been. The study of the textual tradition of the catholic letters reveals that several commentary manuscripts stand at important places in the transmission of the text.[40] Thus to exclude all catena manuscripts would be to lose some extremely valuable information about the history of the text. At the same time manuscripts of other catena types conform to the Byzantine norm. The manuscripts of Euthymius Zigabenus' catena agree at very nearly 100 per cent with the Majority Text at the test passages in John 1–10.

There is one further problem with the situation as we have inherited it. If we return to the manuscript lists in the discussion of MS Vallicelliana E.40 (Tables 2.1 and 2.2), it will be noted that one of these manuscripts (Vatican, Barb. gr. 504, Gregory-Aland 849), has already been mentioned. It is one of the five copies of Cyril of Alexandria's Commentary on John which I said should not be in the *Liste* at all.[41] Citations of Cyril should be included among the patristic citations, with a note if necessary to indicate that there is variation between the manuscripts. What we must not do is report the evidence twice, once as a Cyrillian citation and once as manuscript

Gregory-Aland 849. But we need to know more here. Are the lemmata in this manuscript part of the Cyrillian tradition? If not, then we should be including the manuscript on its intrinsic value. If they are, then perhaps we should still be including the manuscript, since its status as a complete text which may shed light on the history of the tradition may be too high for it to be broken into individual citations. How does it compare with the text as it is reported in the standard edition of Cyril's commentary, and how reliable is that edition? Whatever the answers to these questions, we will certainly be ill-advised to exclude the evidence of this manuscript, however we choose to record it.[42]

It is very interesting to ask why it is that some catena manuscripts occupy such an important position in the transmission of the text. It is a question currently occupying the mind of a Birmingham PhD student (Michael Clark), and we await his discoveries with interest.

The situation is this: we find that while every logical rule of systematic classification of evidence requires us to throw these catena manuscripts overboard, the textual evidence that has, admittedly rather chaotically, happened to have been gathered implores us to hold on to them.

The editor of the New Testament is therefore confronted by a weakness in the available data. In an ideal world, we should start again with studying the commentary manuscripts and draw up clearer criteria for including them. Once a more comprehensive list has been drawn up, the manuscripts should be categorized according to catena type, and the New Testament text should be tested to establish the textual groupings. For the moment, we have to acknowledge that the scholars of the late nineteenth century and the first part of the twentieth went in the wrong direction with the commentary manuscripts, and it will take a while to establish a better situation. In the short term, the process of editing the New

Testament will just have to continue with the materials it has available, while developing separately a research programme reassessing the catena manuscripts.

Let us remember that we are trying to answer the question 'What is a New Testament manuscript?' I illustrate the difficulties with regard to commentary manuscripts by drawing attention to the completely different situation that obtains with the most important witness to Origen's commentary on John (M, Codex Monacensis 191). It has a large lacuna between the end of Book VI (in which Origen discusses 1.29) and the beginning of Book X, which starts with 2.12. This gap is imperfectly filled by the continuous text (contrary to Origen's normal custom) of the whole of Chapter 2. This block of text is therefore not a part of Origen's text, and has instead a right to be treated as a witness to the text of the Greek manuscript from which it is derived. So, if the commentaries become dubious witnesses because they do not contain the continuous text, it could equally be argued that this passage (which is discounted from evidence for the text of Origen on obvious grounds) deserves its very own Gregory-Aland number. As it is, its witness is currently excluded both from the analysis of New Testament manuscripts and from the study of Origen's text. It inhabits a sort of unquiet shadowland of unbaptized manuscripts.

Liturgical books and lectionary manuscripts

A variety of books are necessary for the liturgy: ones containing the texts of the liturgy itself, and copies of works used within it, such as hymns and readings from the Bible. The Psalms and biblical Odes were often copied as a separate collection. For example, Vienna, Österreichische Nationalbibliothek Pap. K 8706 (Gregory-Aland P42), the single remaining sheet of a codex, contains the end of the Magnificat (Luke 1.54–5) and the Nunc Dimittis (Luke 2.29–32).[43] Codex Alexandrinus (London, British Library Royal Ms. 1 D.VIII) contains the Odes, which includes the canticles from Luke 1 and 2, and thus has these texts twice.

A lectionary contains the biblical text rearranged according to the order of the church's year. These manuscripts are the least studied of all, since the textual critics have paid little attention to them. Yet it is worth observing that from the eleventh century on it was the lectionary that was the 'Gospel book' par excellence, the 'Evangelion', while a new word, the 'Tetraevangelion', was found for the continuous-text copy.

Since the lectionary contains the same text as a continuous-text manuscript, just in a different order, it might be thought that our interest here is not with content but with genre and function. But in fact content, genre, and function are inseparable. Once we begin to study liturgical books, the division between copies of New Testament works and service books becomes uncertain. Biblical sentences, Psalms, or phrases from Psalms are also lections, but lections which have become more fully embedded in the texture of the liturgy. One may see this exemplified in the database of Latin patristic citations of the Bible. Lections are treated as biblical manuscripts. Shorter excerpts are treated as biblical citations. Thus the Old Latin manuscript 34, the Lectio Cryptoferratensis (Grottaferrata, Biblioteca della Badia Γ.β.VI) contains John 1.1–17.[44] On the other hand, Johannine text in manuscripts of the various rites—the Mozarabic, the Gallican, and so on—are treated as patristic citations. To illustrate the confusion, another entry classified as an Old Latin manuscript (Verona, Biblioteca Capitolare LI (49), fol. 19v, number 49 in the Beuron list of Old Latin biblical manuscripts), known as the Lectio Veronensis, consists of John 12.12–13a added in the margin of a sermon. These examples, which incidentally show us that the difficulties of classification which we have already encountered among Greek manuscripts also belong to those in other languages, draw our attention to the fact that with both catena manuscripts and lectionary manuscripts we are faced with a fundamental question about the process of classifying documents and texts according to the heading of works. The question is, can it be satisfactory?

With regard to the lectionaries, the question has to be asked again, as it was for the catena manuscripts, whether it is appropriate to treat them in the same way as the plain continuous-text manuscripts. On the face of it, again the answer no seems rather compelling. But again, if we want to trace the textual history of the works with which we are concerned, then there is a similar justification for including them. If lectionaries were copied only from other lectionaries, then this independent textual tradition could be separately analysed, and only the evidence concerning the text of the prior continuous-text manuscripts would be of interest in editing the text. But this may not necessarily be how the lectionaries were produced. Recent research by Chris Jordan has proposed the working hypothesis that lectionaries were not always copied from existing lectionaries, but were on at least some occasions freshly compiled from continuous-text manuscripts.[45] It is certainly strange that section divisions which one might expect to be unique either to continuous or to lectionary manuscripts are found in both.[46] If this is the case, then textually we cannot expect lectionaries to group into their own text types. Instead, they should reflect the variety and groupings of the continuous-text manuscripts, and provide information about the development of the text. As with the catena manuscripts, they might even help us to fill in some gaps.

In one respect the lectionaries offer better opportunities for analysis than the continuous-text manuscripts, since Jordan has shown that they may be classified according to the sequence of their lections as well as according to their textual character. This and any material identifying readings for special occasions (such as a saint with a local repute) may also help to locate the place of origin of a manuscript.

More recently, a detailed examination of one manuscript in the Metropolitan Museum of Art (the Jaharis Lectionary) has made a plausible case not only that it was created in Constantinople, but that it was intended for a very specific liturgical purpose in Hagia Sophia.[47] To be precise, the liturgy for certain events required that a Gospel book be placed on the Patriarch's throne. It was not opened to be read. It was placed there. This example gives the intriguing possibility that the manuscript was copied, not to be *read*, but simply so that it should exist. In this respect its function is analogous to that of an amulet. One wonders whether it follows that it was never copied, and therefore represents a complete dead end in the textual transmission.

Paratext: the Euthalian Apparatus

In addition to the biblical and commentary texts already discussed, there is another type of material in the manuscripts to which I will briefly refer. This is the various systems of introductions, lists of quotations, and explanations accompanying different books. The best example is the so-called Euthalian Apparatus to Acts and the epistles.[48] As originally developed, this system included sense-division and punctuation of the text, for better presentation of the sense in public reading. Thus the manuscripts with the Euthalian Apparatus contained the biblical text in a very distinctive form with regard both to layout and to explanatory material. We have to ask whether by wresting the apostolic text of such manuscripts out of their sophisticated environment of text and paratext, with levels of script, we are not doing harm to our understanding by ripping the jewel out of its setting. Moreover, a study of a text within its whole environment in the manuscript containing it may provide further evidence for placing it within the tradition.

Paratext: chapter titles

Finally, there is the status of chapter numberings, headings, and systems. I take the example of three Latin lectionary manuscripts containing prefatory canon tables with titles of the sections.[49] These titles contain Old Latin forms of the text, although the lectionaries themselves are Vulgate. Once again, we have a problem of classification. We may say that the document contains several works: one is the Gospel of John; another is a set of titles to the Gospel of John. This second work also happens to contain some of the Gospel of John, but with another text from the first. Or is it better to describe the second work as another version of the Gospel of John? Either way, we are again in a situation similar to that which we noted in discussing commentaries, where the text of the lemma and the text of the author's running citations may differ. The similarity is close enough that in the Vetus Latina edition of John we have taken the decision to treat these three 'manuscripts' as patristic citations.[50]

Non-textual elements

Textual scholars are obsessed with textual data. They have come to ignore other elements in a document. In many though, the most striking elements to the casual eye are decorative: portraits of evangelists, decorative headbands, illuminated initial letters, ornate canon tables. These are as much a part of their manuscripts as the text which they adorn (or even force it into second place). I will have more to say about this in the next lecture. For the present I only ask the question whether the text must necessarily be our only criterion for classifying manuscripts.

Conclusions

To sum up: I have discussed papyrus manuscripts, and the difficulties of distinguishing between purpose, contents, and function. I then moved onto the question of canonicity, looking at the Bodmer Miscellaneous Codex and the oldest parchment Bibles. Next I described the complexities and confusions surrounding the catena manuscripts, and dealt more briefly with the lectionaries and various kinds of paratext.

Let us step back from the groups of manuscripts which have so far been discussed, and ask what we have learned.

1. It seems clear that in the period since the first detailed lists of witnesses began to be made by Gregory in his completion of Tischendorf's eighth edition, compilers have differed in their views on what should be included. Thus some categories (talismans and ostraca) have come and gone, some have been only partially recorded (catena manuscripts), and some (inscriptions) have never been included.

2. It is also obvious that the cataloguing system is rather inadequate. In fact we probably have to acknowledge that no system will work perfectly and that there will always be anomalies.

3. In terms of the older manuscripts, we have difficulty in knowing what kind of materials we are dealing with. Some of them seem to serve purposes not very closely related to what we would consider normal reading of the text. But even such documents, be they amulets or made for uncertain purposes, can be valuable witnesses for the purpose of studying the early history of the New Testament.

4. The situation with regard to the commentary manuscripts is far more problematical. The established list catalogues 250 manuscripts of John's Gospel. Reuss' researches in a few libraries unearthed another thirty-eight. There may be many more.

5. The lectionaries suffer from a similar difficulty, in that they cannot be fully distinguished from other kinds of service books. But they cannot easily be neglected if we want to understand the history of the text as fully as possible.

The time has come to ask again the question 'What is a New Testament Manuscript?'

The answer requires an adjustment in our categories. The unsatisfactory situation I have described depends on four classes which are all in some way inconsistent. The criteria consist of:

Material:	papyrus and parchment, but with no category for paper
Script:	majuscule and minuscule, but with no mixed categories
Structure:	continuous text or lectionary, but with no category for commentaries or excerpts such as talismans
Work:	New Testament, with all other works that may be in any given manuscript totally ignored, and with only limited recording of the many works of which the New Testament is composed

[handwritten annotation: A Bible with the NT, + except the Gospels & Revelation]

This classification has arisen out of the traditional way of making a list, which involves a sheet of paper and a writing implement. In this system, and when the first lists began to be made, it seemed so simple: a copy of the Gospels here, a Praxapostolos there and we begin to list the Greek New Testament manuscripts. We must remember that the principal object of this classifying has been to find the material from which to make a critical edition. Thus, manuscripts have been listed on the grounds that they comply somehow with the requirements of a modern edition of the twenty-seven books in the Greek and Western canon of the New Testament. However, the risk arises that in pursuing this goal we not only twist and neglect information, but insist on an inappropriate goal. Let us step back from the requirements of the critical edition, and look at it from the point of view of the manuscripts. What else could we say about them if we could start *describing* them all over again? In the first place, would we want to use the four categories of material, script, structure, and work? The answer is: no. Would we want to subdivide them at all? Possibly not, but if we did one might consider the two basic categories of continuous text or non-continuous. We would certainly want to include some other important information, such as a manuscript's Sitz im Leben (in two senses for the Jaharis Lectionary) and a record of *all* the works within a particular manuscript.

But, do we want to start all over again with a new list and new numbers? Doing the same thing again in another way would surely create a lot of confusion and endless problems.[51] The answer is surely no. And there is no reason why we should. We are no longer dependent on paper lists.

The database offers far more possibilities for describing manuscripts. And in fact the use of multiple fields, which may be displayed or hidden or rearranged according to the user's purposes, offers a better analogy for describing the early Christian and Byzantine codex, which could be adapted to a variety of contents, formats, purposes, and uses. We can keep the traditional system, but by adding fields and search and sort facilities we can recover from them much more helpful kinds of information. Where a document contains multiple works, it can appear in more than one database (or one would provide multiple views of a single database). Thus the Bodmer Miscellaneous Codex can appear in several lists based on work, a commentary manuscript in two, and a catena manuscript in many more. We can also catalogue a four-Gospel manuscript under the contents categories of the collections New Testament and Gospels and under each individual work.

With genre and function categories we can include amulets, marginalia, inscriptions, ostraca, and citations, and distinguish between copies we want to include in a critical edition and those we do not.

We can also include further information about layout and artwork and make links to other sites and images which will enrich the bald statements of the database.

We can catalogue catena manuscripts and even odd bits of other manuscripts such as Codex Monacensis 191 under the twin genres of New Testament work(s) and the catena, and for good measure if we needed to we could abstract the individual citations by a father (such as John Chrysostom) and link them to a database of patristic citations.

In the end, the database of copies will not be a free-standing database, but a way of linking transcriptions, images, and metadata. The Virtual Manuscript Room in Münster has already begun to offer data in a different format from the printed list, aided by the opportunity to include images and transcriptions. The Birmingham Virtual Manuscript Room, which is not limited to Greek New Testament manuscripts, offers the opportunity to make connections across textual boundaries. This will provide us with a variety of ways of finding the kind of material we want, depending on our starting point.[52]

So we are back with the question: When is a manuscript a copy of the New Testament, and when is it not? The answer is that in so far as it is based upon our own research purposes rather than on the nature of the manuscripts, this is the wrong question. In fact in both antiquity and the Byzantine world there was scarcely any such thing as a copy of the New Testament.[53] Let us try to formulate a different way of thinking about the problem.

The modern concept of a New Testament manuscript is based upon the theological model of canonicity. As is well known, the idea of a canon emerged over the course of many years, and the list with which we are familiar was first given by Athanasius in his Thirty-Ninth Festal Letter, written in 367. Until then there evidently could not be any manuscript whose contents intentionally corresponded to this list, and in fact there is precious little evidence that many copies did so for centuries thereafter, and rarely then until the advent of printing. Even when Greek-speaking Christianity came to agree a canon, it did not really occur to anyone that such a canon should be the basis for the contents of a manuscript. So we may say that the concept of the canon works only at the level of the collection of works. It does not function very well at the level of the text, and hardly at all at that of the document. The process of listing manuscripts (in a database, of course) has therefore to start with the proper description of the full contents of the manuscript. An editor will subsequently be able to single out the copies appropriate to be included in an edition. We may conclude that the best way to list all the copies of a single work is to make a complete database of all manuscripts of every work.[54]

This approach is a particular way of following the suggestion I made in the first lecture, that 'every written work is a process and not an object', which sets it in the context of the hierarchy of documents, texts, and work which I also discussed. If we apply the idea that a text is a process to the idea of a canon of books, then a new approach emerges. This approach considers not the canonicity of a work, but the canonicity of a document. A document may contain a mixture of canonical and non-canonical texts. This is evidently true of Codex Sinaiticus, Codex Alexandrinus, and the Bodmer Miscellaneous Codex. It is also true of every manuscript classified as containing the Greek New Testament which has a catena. Once we begin not with texts but with documents, we discover that there is a whole grey world of manuscripts lurking on the edge of canonicity. It is evident enough that some of the more extensive papyri with a Gregory-Aland number contain canonical texts, such as the three Chester Beatty manuscripts of the Gospels and Acts, Paul, and Revelation, and the two Bodmer papyri of the Gospels. Likewise, there are plenty of Byzantine manuscripts which contain virtually nothing but canonical text. But if we look at the full range of manuscripts generally listed as containing the New Testament, we find that a very high number contain significant amounts of non-canonical text. This leads me to consider what is probably the most fundamental question with regard to the written New Testament, namely its position within the entire tradition of Christian belief. The comparatively straightforward copies of canonical texts, the amulets, the ostraca, the inscriptions, the commentary manuscripts, the canon tables, the lectionaries, the tools for the user, are all parts of the way in which the Gospels, Praxapostolos, and Apocalypse have been read, heard, transmitted, and scrutinized. The written texts have no independent function, but are one part of a never-ending sequence of conversations, arguments, and interpretations.

We may illustrate this by considering an example of the degree to which the tradition becomes layered in manuscripts. Thus a citation from the Septuagint contained in a New Testament work may be found embedded in a Greek New Testament manuscript. In the catena tradition this may happen at a number of layers. What should one make of a citation from the Septuagint contained in a New Testament work which is cited by John Chrysostom which is then excerpted into a catena, and copied a number of times in the manuscript tradition of that catena? It is presumably a part of all those works. But such repetition calls into question the uniqueness of the individual works, which may only differ in degree from the uniqueness of individual copies of a work.

The written text was a convenient tool in the transmission of beliefs and ideas and shared information. To us it is more important because it comprises most of the remaining evidence. But because they are almost all that has survived, the manuscripts are now divorced from their original setting. Nevertheless, since conversations, arguments, and interpretations have never ceased, these copies from the past remain a part of the process to which we too belong.

At this point I realize that what I am propounding is that there is no such thing as a manuscript of the New Testament. The New Testament is not a work but a collection of works. I wish I had realized this before writing a book called *An Introduction to the New Testament Manuscripts and their Texts*. Instead, I propose that we should begin to classify manuscripts according to the basic categories of works. This could usefully include categories that were available to the world in which the manuscripts were made. At the earliest period, the available category will have been of individual works. Thus, it has been argued that Gospel books at Oxyrhynchus contained only a single Gospel. Later, the category of a Tetraevangelion emerged.[55] Probably the next step in making the New Testament is to acknowledge that the concept 'New Testament' does not help us to understand the Greek manuscripts.

The concept of the text as a process implies that there is a sequential connection between each small step in the process. Philologists have generally thought so, and have tried to express the connection as connections between manuscripts and states of the text. This topic will be my subject in the next lecture, when I discuss how manuscripts are related.

THIRD LECTURE

UNDERSTANDING HOW MANUSCRIPTS ARE RELATED

With long poring, he is grown almost into a book.

Charles Lamb, 'Oxford in the Vacation'

Understanding how manuscripts are related is an attempt to create a narrative. I finished the previous lecture by discussing the place of the written text within the process of human activity which is the Christian tradition. The manuscripts, along with other products such as buildings and paintings, are more or less the only tangible survivors of early Christian discourse still available to us. We have to remember that a great deal more of it, namely people's daily lives, social activities, and spoken words, is lost to us and survives only in so far as it is echoed in the words which we speak today. We seek to understand the entire tradition by studying what survives, a significant part of which consists of the process of textual transmission, the copying of a new manuscript from an old one, which in turn was itself copied. Inasmuch as this process has been affected by the sequence of generations through which it has passed, the works themselves are survivors in the form of texts received, and passed on time and again.

The study of this process has taken its own particular form, so that it is in some ways unlike other aspects of research in the humanities.

It has one advantage and one disadvantage. The advantage is that it deals with hard data, namely the actual differences between the manuscripts, which may be observed, described, and quantified. The disadvantage is that the hardness of the data may obscure the softness of the conclusions drawn from it. Everyone in humanities research depends upon the editions produced by the textual scholars. Everyone should know the value of the editions as evidence for the age to which the work they seek to recreate belongs.

Subscribers to the papyrology e-list received a timely reminder of this recently, in the form of a quotation from B. J. Kemp's book *Ancient Egypt: Anatomy of a Civilization*:

the more I try to make sense of the facts, the more what I write is speculative and begins to merge with the world of historical fiction, a modern form of myth.[1]

The philologists need to consider what other narrative or further purpose our scholarship serves, but this is a topic I will leave aside for the moment. What we are concerned with now is the initial stages of gathering some facts and then beginning to make sense of them. I repeat my observation in the first lecture that it is not self-evident that we need to study a manuscript tradition in order to trace it back to its roots. One might also suppose that it is reasonable to argue that a textual tradition improves as it develops. This is a point of view in Orthodox Christianity, in which the text is revered as it has been passed on within the Church's tradition. To those who regard this as a hallowed history, the findings of a modern philologist may seem rather less weighty. The idea that a text becomes better with time can also be viewed as an extension of the initial creative process into its later history. The author of a work today, after all, sketches and drafts and revises until the work seems satisfactory, or time runs out, or boredom sets in. After that the copy-editor and then the proofreader will add further improvements, and a printed text will appear. But why should the improvement of the text stop there? A reader may correct misprints and add marginal observations. Is not that a better text, at least if the corrections do not make it worse and the observations are informed? If this is true of a printed work, is it not necessarily equally true of a manuscript tradition, in which the divisions between author and reader, autograph and copy are much less clear? We may see evidence to support this view with regard to the Greek New Testament in the many places where solecisms have been corrected. Such variants demonstrate that a degree of editing continued for many centuries. And there were fierce debates about such questions—for example, the argument in the second century with regard to the propriety of Atticizing a Hellenistic text.

If we do believe that the text got better, then we will still be interested in seeing how it developed, but in order to find out what it became, not how it began. Such an inquiry will also be as interested in ways in which it did not change as in ways in which it did.

There is a third approach to the comparison of manuscripts whose goal is neither to trace the manuscript tradition back to its roots nor to seek its Byzantine apotheosis. It may be equally important to travel hopefully without seeking to arrive, by comparing different forms of a work in order to study the ways in which it developed and the various forms to which its interpretation and use led. This is certainly the case with regard to the Acts of the Apostles, which was preserved in one fairly fixed form and also in a variety of rather freely developing versions.[2] Is it fanciful to explain the free versions as a response to the genre of the work, which it has been argued resembles a Hellenistic novel?[3] While the fixed form may be more help in reconstructing both the older versions and the way in which Byzantine forms appeared, it is in a study of the variety of ways in which it was transmitted that we learn most about the variety of ways in which the work was regarded in antiquity.

These questions of purpose will be considered again in the fourth and fifth lectures. Having noted them, we now turn to the comparison of manuscripts. We need to remember still the distinction between documents, texts, and works. What concerns us most closely now is the interaction of information about documents and information about the texts written in them. When here I speak about the relationship between manuscripts, I have in mind either one or both of the document and the text. Inasmuch as a text is accurate, it reproduces a text older than the manuscript in which it is written. If two texts differed more than they agreed, one would have to question the view that they represented the same work. It therefore also follows that all texts of a work agree more than they differ. Understanding this, and finding ways of quantifying the agreement as well as the disagreement, is an important and undervalued aspect of the recent computer-aided methodologies developed for the study of the New Testament.

What are the ways of understanding how manuscripts are related? There are three approaches to be considered, each with its own kind of evidence. These are:

- physical evidence for close relationship;
- comparison of artwork, including miniatures, decorative bands, other embellishments and coronae;
- analysis of the text.

Out of all the manuscripts we have, it is comparatively rare to be able to find physical evidence of a relationship, so this kind of analysis is not always available. Not all manuscripts have any kind of artwork, and we can only compare those which do. The one thing which all our manuscripts have in common is that they contain text.[4] It is therefore not surprising that it is upon the text that most attempts to relate manuscripts to one another are based. I will have most to say about these attempts, but will say something first about the other two. I will take each in turn as the starting point of the section, and then expand on the contribution of the other two approaches to the examples I choose.

Physical evidence

It is not common (yet at any rate) to be able to establish a connection between two or more manuscripts on the grounds of shared physical attributes. No doubt there are many connections waiting to be made, if only we were able to gather information and then to take the time to study it. In the broadest possible terms, of course, we can date a manuscript within a fifty-year period, which necessarily involves comparison with other manuscripts. It is also possible, for example, to recognize a south Italian hand and to consider that there may be further historical connections between south Italian copies of a work.[5] But these are rather general preliminary observations. What we are looking for is evidence that one manuscript has been copied from another, or that several were written in the same place at the same time. Any physical connection will do. One good place to start is by finding two or more manuscripts written by the same scribe. I take three examples to illustrate the possibilities and difficulties of finding such evidence.

Theodoros Hagiopetrites

First, the scribe Theodoros Hagiopetrites, whose dated manuscripts span the thirty years between 1278 and 1308. He copied at least twelve manuscripts containing some part of the New Testament.[6] Some are dated, so that we may produce the chronology:

1278   Copenhagen, Kongelige Bibliotek GKS 1322, 4° (Gregory-Aland 234), Gospels and Praxapostolos

1280   Vatican gr. 644 (Gregory-Aland 856),[7] Theophylact's Gospel commentary

1284   Athos, Vatopedi 962 (Gregory-Aland 1594), Gospels and Praxapostolos

1292   London, British Library Burney 21 (Gregory-Aland 484), Gospels and Praxapostolos

1301   Athos, Pantokrator 47 (Gregory-Aland 1394), Gospels

1301   Venice, Biblioteca Nazionale Marciana I.19 (1416) (Gregory-Aland 412), Gospels[8]

The Burney manuscript is available in its entirety among the British Library's digital library of Greek manuscripts, and is the best place to examine his work in physical detail. We know a certain amount about Hagiopetrites: that he lived and worked in Thessaloniki, that he was a lector, and that he had a daughter called Eirene who was also a scribe. His manuscripts have been described from the art historical point of view by Robert Nelson, who has shown that Hagiopetrites did most of his own artwork, and there have also been studies of the text. We can build on these with our fuller sets of textual data.

One might speculate whether Hagiopetrites used manuscripts with a similar form of text as his exemplars. It would be too much to hope that he ever used the same manuscript twice. But to follow this up we need to compare the texts of the manuscripts. A comparison of textual data in test passages in the Gospels reveals that none of these manuscripts is very close, except for two pairs. The more striking relationship is between the two copied in 1301. They agree in 151 out of 153 test passages in John 1–10.[9] If we work back through the Gospels comparing the test passage results, we find a similarly close relationship in Luke, where they have 100 per cent agreement in the 54 test passages (interestingly, with two other manuscripts).[10] One would expect the same situation to apply in Matthew and Mark, leading us to the satisfying conclusion that these two manuscripts had either been copied from the same antegraph or the one was copied from the other. It is rather disappointing therefore to find that the situation is dramatically different in the first half. In Matthew there are no indications that they are particularly closely related, and in fact the Pantokrator manuscript (1394) has a high degree of agreement with a number of other copies; the same is true in Mark.[11] Thus the two texts differ most at the beginning and least at the end of the Gospels. One explanation for this might be that after one copy had been made, the exemplar had been corrected prior to a second copying, the corrector steadily losing interest before the end. At this stage one may say that the enquiry, which began with a list of manuscripts by the same scribe, yields some contradictory and intriguing preliminary conclusions.

I note finally that the two manuscripts are not dissimilar in format. According to the *Liste*, they have the following dimensions:

	Venice	Athos
pages	329	335
columns	1	1
lines	22	21
dimensions	17.7 × 13	23.5 × 17

The one is in a larger format than the other, but the page layout and resultant number of leaves is strikingly similar. It might be that Theodore was either imitating the format of the same exemplar or following the same calculation for adopting his own format.

The other interesting pairing is made by the Copenhagen and Vatopedi manuscripts (Gregory-Aland 234 and 1594). They agree in all the 196 test passages in Mark with one small variation. But then seven other manuscripts also show the same level of agreement with these two. In John they are also very close, but in Matthew and Luke there is no similar affinity. We are left again wondering what this amounts to, and how such a pattern of greater similarity in Mark and John than in Matthew and Luke may be explained.

Many further lines of research are prompted by this brief inquiry. What we have learned is that the physical and historical evidence concerning the documents is a valuable way of testing the textual data, which on its own can be either incomplete or misleading, and of constructing more sophisticated models of the relationship between copies. We have also learned that the different lines of inquiry do not necessarily provide a road to consistent conclusions.

Ephraim

My second example is a well-known one, and concerns the monk Ephraim, who worked in Constantinople and copied a number of important manuscripts in the middle of the tenth century. These include two sets of works from the New Testament, a Gospel book (Athos, Vatopediu 949, Gregory-Aland 1582) and a Praxapostolos (Athos, Laura B´ 64, Gregory-Aland 1739). What is most striking about Ephraim's work is the quality of his exemplars and his care in reproducing the marginal comments preserved in the tradition he is copying. It transpires that his Gospels are a key witness to the distinctive and ancient textual tradition known as Family 1, while the other volume is scarcely less precious. Purely textual research has revealed the existence of Family 1, but a knowledge of Ephraim's other work and something of his life allows us to observe in detail the best of Byzantine textual scholarship. The fact that he seems to have been able to locate and recognize significant copies not only of New Testament works but also of writers such as Aristotle is an important factor in appraising the textual value of his copies.

Codex Sinaiticus and Codex Vaticanus

My final example is far more speculative, and deals with our two most important fourth-century manuscripts, Codex Sinaiticus and Codex Vaticanus. It was maintained even by Tischendorf that the two manuscripts have a scribe in common.[12] Codex Sinaiticus is generally agreed to have had three scribes, known as A, B, and D. Codex Vaticanus was copied by two, A and B. According to Tischendorf, Scribe D of Codex Sinaiticus was identical with Scribe B of Codex Vaticanus.[13] Subsequently, Milne and Skeat reached the conclusion that Scribe D of Codex Sinaiticus had more in common with the *other* scribe of Codex Vaticanus, Scribe A.[14] In their analysis of the hands of the Sinaiticus, they reached the conclusion that the decorative designs in the colophons supplied the best evidence for distinguishing the hands. On this basis, they noted what they regarded as a remarkable similarity between Scribe D's colophon to Mark in Codex Sinaiticus and the colophon drawn by Scribe A of Vaticanus at the end of Deuteronomy. How similar are they? At a glance, very. But after a few moments one may suggest these differences:

There is a space above the colophon in Sinaiticus.

The two devices occupy different positions in the column.

The horizontal decorations extend to the right margin in Sinaiticus.

The word is on one line in Vaticanus, but split across two in Sinaiticus.

The presentation is better balanced in Sinaiticus; in Vaticanus the word is not centred.

In sum, it may be said that the visual conceptualization differs.[15] The similarity is likely to be in the eye of the beholder.

I remain sceptical with regard to all attempts to find a close relationship between these two manuscripts, let alone between two of their scribes. I suspect that they look so similar to our eyes only because there are no other manuscripts very similar to either of them, since there are no other fourth-century Bibles still in existence. The attempt thus serves as a warning that we must try to resist the temptation to find connections everywhere and to try to create a complete picture out of the few surviving fragments of the fourth-century manuscript tradition. The further back we go into a period from which virtually no manuscripts survive, the less precise our connections will be and the greater the distance between the surviving copies. We will find later on that what we see here with regard to the scripts of the manuscripts applies also to their texts.

Artwork

The role of art history has been largely neglected by textual scholarship, simply because (as I suggested in the first lecture) textual scholars have only studied the text and ignored the other components of a manuscript. This is a serious limitation in our research to date: one of the leading questions, and one that has never been properly addressed, is the degree to which the groupings and affiliations observed when manuscripts are examined for their artwork match groupings proposed by the palaeographical and textual approaches. The advantages of including art history, apart from the fact that it offers a check on these approaches, is that a proper comparison with text-critical findings has the potential to shed a great deal of light on the way in which manuscripts were produced and circulated. The comparison with palaeographical study would shed light on the relationship between scriptoria and artists' workshops, an essential element in reaching a better understanding of Byzantine books. We saw in looking at Hagiopetrites some of the possibilities (and difficulties) of such a combined approach.

A start has been made in this kind of analysis and comparison with the decorative style, which has been studied in detail by Annemarie Weyl Carr.[16] Current in the period 1150–1250, this style is found in more than a hundred manuscripts. They can be divided into a number of subgroups, purely on the basis of their illuminations. The subgroups can be attributed at least partially to specific locations, such as Cyprus. Textual scholarship has generally been attracted by the thesis that texts copied in a particular place developed their own characteristics, just as species of plants and animals do.[17] On these grounds one might suppose that all manuscripts shown by their artwork to have been written in Cyprus must share textual characteristics not found in other manuscripts. But some preliminary research by Maxwell suggests that the picture is nothing like as simple as this.[18] There are good examples of pairs or groups of manuscripts with similar illuminations and similar texts, in fact that seem to be closely related in every respect, so that they are likely to be from the same area, place, or even scriptorium. It can also transpire that manuscripts with clear textual affinities turn out to share nothing in terms of other characteristics such as format, script, and miniatures, and vice versa.

The use of such art historical evidence by textual scholars is in its infancy. Jordan, in his research on lectionaries began to use it, and Maxwell and researchers working on the *Editio critica maior* are starting to take significant steps towards pooling their expertise.[19] At the Society of Biblical Literature annual congress in San Francisco in November 2011 there was a session dedicated to 'A Holistic Approach to Two Contemporary Purple Parchment Gospel Books: St Petersburg, National Library of Russia Gr. 53 (Gregory-Aland 565) and Tirana, Beratinus 2 (Gregory-Aland 1143)', in which there were presentations by textual scholars (Bruce Morrill and Ulrich Schmid), an art historian (Kathleen Maxwell), and a palaeographer (Nadezhda Kavrus-Hoffmann). The session demonstrated an important point: that scholarship cannot be advanced by individuals trying to become expert in several fields. The way forward is in collaboration.

Textual analysis

There is clearly much more work to be done in studying the physical and art historical elements in the manuscripts. The same is true of textual analysis, but compared to the other two it has a longer history and has been more systematically undertaken. It is on this aspect that I will concentrate for the remainder of this lecture. I will say something about the development of methodologies, and then will talk about the most important model for describing the relationship between texts. I hope that it now goes without saying that the other approaches must not be forgotten. But in order to underline the point, I offer these three requirements for any model.

1. The model should be based upon consistent analysis of as complete a collection of data as possible. I will give in a moment examples of extremely influential arguments which are based upon very small amounts of data. Today we can and should do better.

2. The model should be transparent, with all the data and all the process of argument open to the user.

3. The model has to be compatible with what we know about the construction of documents, the copying of texts, and the history of the work in question, at each point in its history. For example, we work, most obviously, on the basis that unless there is evidence to the contrary a copy of a text will have been made by one scribe from another single copy. But we will have to bear in mind that on occasion two copies may have been used, or two scribes may have been at work. We may need to consider whether a work was produced to dictation or by copying. We will have to remember that a scribe may have had a mental text which sometimes drove out the written text being copied.

The history of manuscript comparison

Ever since the eighteenth century, the textual history of the New Testament has been described by grouping manuscripts. The person credited with first setting out the idea is J. A. Bengel (1687–1752), who in 1734 classified all Greek New Testament manuscripts as either Asiatic or African. This theory ascribes a geographical explanation to textual similarity. It is important to remember that Bengel only needed to find a theory to explain the relationship between a mere sixteen manuscripts.[20] As more manuscripts were found and studied, his approach was further developed by J. S. Semler (1725–91),

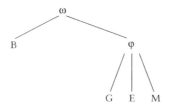

Figure 3.1: Lachmann's stemma of manuscripts of *Das Nibelungenlied* (after Timpanaro, simplified)

and then by J. J. Griesbach (1745–1812), who divided the witnesses into three groups.[21]

According to the received wisdom, the most significant advance in finding a way of stating the relationship between manuscripts was offered by Karl Lachmann (1793–1851), whose theory of stemmatology included the reconstruction of a family tree. Figure 3.1 gives an example from his study of a German text.[22]

Such a 'rooted tree' shows how the manuscripts relate to the starting point of the textual tradition. The construction is based upon the process of comparing variant readings, establishing the point in the process at which new forms arose and thus by elimination reconstructing the oldest text. But as Timpanaro demonstrated in *The Genesis of Lachmann's Method*, the concept of a stemma long pre-dates Lachmann. In fact he attributes its origins to Bengel.[23] In his words, Bengel

imagined that in the distant future the whole history of the New Testament tradition could be summarised in a *tabula genealogica*, that is, in what will later come to be called a *stemma codicum*.[24]

Bengel's conception has been concealed by the fact that he produced nothing like the diagrammatic stemma with which we are familiar from more recent work, and by the way in which New Testament textual scholarship continued to use his terminology but came to ignore his intentions.

Further on Bengel repeats even more explicitly that it is the consensus of manuscripts *belonging to different families* that guarantees the antiquity of a reading.[25]

We thus see in Bengel the situation that continued in New Testament textual scholarship until almost the present day, in which genealogical theory has been expressed by grouping manuscripts. Where the Asiatic and the African families agree, they must represent the form of text from which both are derived. To put it differently, where the manuscripts differ, the reading which is found in copies belonging to each family is to be preferred, since it must pre-date the split between them. Any reading found in only one family must post-date that split. That looks simple. But we can imagine two possibilities that would cast doubt on the procedure. The first is if there were two variants, each supported by members of each family. The second is that it presupposes that the two families remained wholly separate from each other after the split had occurred. While this view might have been sustainable when only sixteen manuscripts were known, the evidence of hundreds of witnesses demonstrates that there was no such separation between the supposed groups.

Bengel's basic methodology has remained in use with hardly any changes. All that happened in later scholarship was that as more manuscripts became known, the classification changed and grew. Thus by the end of the nineteenth century there were Western, Syrian, and Alexandrian texts. In the twentieth century and as a result of the discovery of more manuscripts, notably the Chester Beatty Gospel papyrus, a Caesarean text of the Gospels was proposed.

Later there began to be talk of a 'proto-Alexandrian' text. One still reads arguments that readings which are attested by a wide geographical spread of witnesses have a good claim to superiority.[26] If I had time, I would want to protest rather strongly against such a view. The geographical range of a reading may show its age or its popularity, but it will not demonstrate its superiority.

So while classical and Germanic philologists developed purer theories to edit their texts, in which genuine stemmata were drawn up, New Testament scholarship never took this step. Why is this? It is often said that the problem with the Lachmannian method is that it has no way of coping with the problem of contamination, in which a particular manuscript (D in the Figure 3.2) has readings derived from another branch of the tradition, perhaps as the result of correction of an earlier copy against such a manuscript.

There is no way of telling which side such a manuscript will come from. A resultant stemma could be either of these.

This is certainly a problem. There is no doubt that the New Testament was copied so often for so long that contamination is everywhere. But in retrospect we can see that a different kind of problem lay behind it. This is the problem of collecting and controlling the necessary data. The Lachmannian method worked by picking

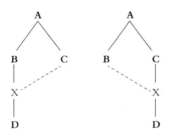

Figure 3.2: Two possible stemmata of a contaminated tradition

out distinctive ('indicative') errors, which constituted a tiny part of the entire wording of the work.[27] Where there are only a few manuscripts and a rather small number of variants, such errors can, with care, be found, and a stemma developed on their foundation. When one comes to deal with the New Testament, however, with so large a number of manuscripts and such a frequency of variant readings, the only thing that becomes clear quickly is that contamination is rife and the situation very complex. Moreover, the frequency of copying meant that the likelihood of an error being made twice independently was rather high, so that errors which would be indicative in another tradition were less trustworthy here.

If success is measured in terms of persuasiveness, then the palm must go to Westcott and Hort, who developed a broad theory to describe the relationships between the groups of manuscripts which scholars had already suggested.[28] They offered a wide historical sweep from the primitive age to the corrupt Byzantine text. The outcome was a theory which classified the manuscripts in three groups, the Alexandrian, the Western, and the Byzantine, with two manuscripts (the codices Vaticanus and Sinaiticus) set apart from the rest as witnesses to a 'Neutral' text. The Alexandrian was a small group of manuscripts from the earlier period regarded as 'the best', and so-called by association with the editorial traditions of Alexandria. The Western witnesses were those which were old and neither conformed to the Alexandrian nor anticipated the Byzantine text, regardless of the fact that they did not have much in common with each other (and were called 'Western' only because of their supposed affinities with the second-century texts known to Irenaeus of Lyons and those found in some Old Latin manuscripts). The vast majority of Greek copies from the seventh century on, comprising perhaps 98 per cent of all known manuscripts, were classed as Byzantine. The three groups are therefore totally different from each other, so that the classification system is hopelessly inconsistent.[29] The best-known diagram of the construct is presented in Streeter's *The Four Gospels*.[30]

But let us pause and scrutinize what Westcott and Hort did a little more carefully. They argued that the Byzantine text of the entire New Testament was secondary to the 'Western' and 'Neutral' traditions on the basis of thirteen readings (pp. 93–107). Apart from the dubious step of applying what is demonstrated for a few books to the entire corpus,[31] we have to say that this is a totally inadequate amount of evidence, even if we grant that their examples are only intended to be exemplary.[32] They did not have the evidential base to substantiate their claim that there is not one contrary example of the conflation found in the Byzantine text. It would be interesting to test their theory, not least their claim that there is not one contrary example, against the full sets of data now available. Their description in summary of the history of the text is this:

Early in the second century we find the Western text already wandering into greater and greater adulteration of the apostolic text, which, while doubtless holding its ground in different places, has its securest refuge at Alexandria; but there in turn it suffers from another but slighter series of changes; and all this before the middle of the third century. At no long time after we find an attempt made, apparently at Antioch, to remedy the growing confusion of texts by the editing of an eclectic text combining readings from the three principal texts, itself further revised on like principles...From that date, and indeed earlier, we find a chaos of varying mixed texts, in which as time advances the elder texts recede, and the Antiochian text now established at Constantinople increasingly prevails. Then even the later types with mixed base disappear, and with the rarest exceptions the Constantinopolitan text alone is copied, often at first with relics of its vanquished rivals included, until at last these too dwindle, and in the copies written shortly before the invention of printing its victory is all but complete. At each stage there are irregularities and obscurities: but we believe the above to be a true sketch of the leading incidents in the history of the text of the New Testament.[33]

The skill with which the picture of a 'wandering' Western text, the 'securest refuge at Alexandria' and the later 'chaos of varying mixed texts' is drawn may keep us from realizing that the evidential basis for this is, throughout, slight. It is almost as remarkable that their Neutral Text, represented by the two manuscripts Sinaiticus and Vaticanus, is placed largely outside this process of change. Subsequent scholarship accepted the textual quality of these two, but preferred to class them as the leading witnesses of the Alexandrian text. What I will concede to be compelling about Westcott and Hort's view is that they describe the textual process so very vividly. Such a strong and simple narrative, with certain indisputable facts, notably the dominance of a single form of text by the time we get to the later Byzantine period, is bound to be attractive. They are not afraid to admit how much 'chaos' lies in the background, and yet they think that this chaos is unable to touch the 'leading incidents'. It is confident and convincing. It has been accepted by most people for a long time. And yet we are left—or should be left—with the feeling that the theory does not deserve the reverence which has been accorded it.

It may seem strange that the methodology first propounded by Bengel has survived down to today. But its virtues are undeniable. It is simple to handle and provides a complete theory and at the same time is flexible so that individual variants can be treated on their own merits. Nevertheless, the time has come to abandon it completely, not because it was wrong, but because we can do better. The main reason why it has lasted, the reason why we have had to wait so long for a successor to Tischendorf and Westcott and Hort, lies in the complexity of the material which has to be described. Any good methodology has to take all the data into account. But with paper and pencil this is impossible. Take the Gospel of John. It is extant in nearly 2,000 manuscripts, which between them probably contain over 11,000 variants. Holding the way these relate to each other, in the hundred or even in the most significant manuscripts, in one's head is beyond any of us. What has changed now is that the database has made it possible to develop a methodology for systematically applying stemmatological principles in a way which keeps the philologist honest. Previously we had to make decisions with unpredictable (in fact with largely unknown) consequences. Now we can make decisions with complex results, and the computer will report those complex results to us. Moreover—and this represents as great a revolution—we are at the same time able to tackle head on the problem of contamination and the problem of the weakened indicative error. We are at last able to make Lachmannian stemmatics workable in complex textual traditions.

The Münster Method

The Münster Method, known formally as the Coherence-Based Genealogical Method, was devised and developed by Gerd Mink, a Mitarbeiter at the Münster Institute who with singular clarity recognized the philological opportunities offered when the data can be recorded and analysed digitally. At one of his earliest presentations, in Birmingham in 1999, it was at once evident that the problem of contamination was a problem no longer. Since then, the method has been greatly developed and refined as it has been applied to editing the Greek New Testament.

It is in essence very simple. It has as its foundation a full list of variants made by comparing complete transcriptions of witnesses.

Where there are many manuscripts (as in the case of the New Testament works), these witnesses are scientifically selected by analysing all known copies in a set of test passages, but where the size of the task is practicable, the inclusion of all witnesses is desirable. The editor studies each unit of variation and where possible produces a stemma showing how the readings developed one from another. This relationship is recorded in a database, in which the relationship between the manuscripts is also recorded and calculated, in particular which is the most likely ancestor of each manuscript. The editor can then ask the database to disclose how all the manuscripts relate to each other. The resulting diagram is described as the textual flow. Let's take an example, using the material available on the internet.[34]

We go to James 1.2, and a simple variant (Figure 3.3). At the top is the editorial text. This is the Initial Text, the text selected by the editors as the form from which all extant texts are descended. There

ἀδελφοί   μου,   ὅταν
8   10   12

11 b   αγαπητοι

Figure 3.3: A variant reading at James 1.2

a) om.
b) αγαπητοι

Figure 3.4: The variant at James 1.2 expressed directionally

is one variant reading, the inclusion of ἀγαπητοί ('beloved') after ἀδελφοί μου ('my brothers').[35]

It is fairly clearly an addition.[36] The relationship between the two readings may be expressed as in Figure 3.4, with an arrow showing the direction of change, what may be called the textual flow (to take the metaphor of a river).[37]

What we see displayed is the readings. The reading a) is always that of the editorial text; b) and all subsequent letters refer to variants from it. We do not need to display the manuscript support. The database will take care of that for us. Of course, we may want to pay attention to the manuscript support, but I do not mention it yet so as to make clear the contribution of the database to understanding the manuscript evidence more fully.

We carry on to make a judgement about the textual history at many points of variation.[38] It is wise to do this first where we are most confident. Examples where it is complex or uncertain should be left aside. As we go on, the relationship between the manuscripts will become ever more complex. When we have made as many decisions as we can, we can ask the database to tell us how our decisions show the manuscripts to be related, either between any two manuscripts, or with regard to all manuscripts. A global reconstruction of all the manuscripts selected for the edition of the catholic letters gathers together the findings of the individual decisions and represents them in a single diagram (Figure 3.5).

We may then go back to each of the local stemmata and see how the overall picture is represented at the local level. Let us look in a little more detail at some of these figures, using the addition at James 1.2. Returning therefore to the apparatus of that variant, we can add the manuscript numbers to the two readings. The added word (reading b) is found in only one witness.[39] In Figure 3.6 the

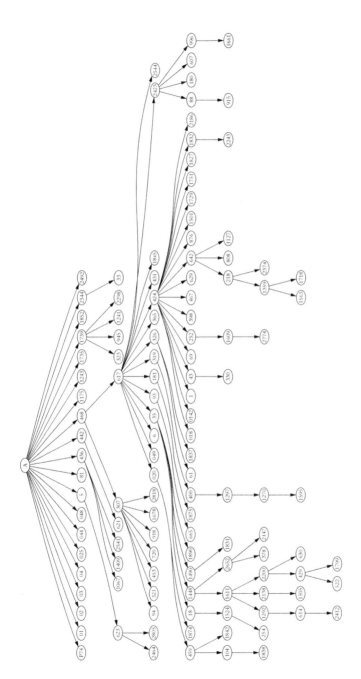

Figure 3.5: The textual flow in the catholic letters of all manuscripts used in the *Editio critica maior*

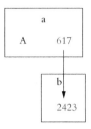

Figure 3.6: The reading at James 1.2, showing the manuscript with reading b and its most probable ancestor

only manuscript given for the first reading is the one indicated in the complete diagram as the most probable ancestor of manuscript 2423.

Using the analytical tools, we can find out why the diagram presents any manuscript as another's most probable ancestor and assess the strength of the evidence. According to the full calculations, the most probable closest ancestor of 2423 is Venice, Biblioteca Nazionale Marciana Gr. Z. 546 (Gregory-Aland 617), an eleventh-century commentary manuscript.[40] This calculation is made on the basis of the sum total of the editors' decisions at the places of variation with regard to the development of the readings.

In the following diagrams, I have omitted from the Münster output several columns containing further information, notably with percentages. I have done this for the sake of sticking to essentials in explaining how the method works. As a result, the numbers in a table do not necessarily add up to the total number of variation units stated.

The tables contain the following information:

A heading stating

1. the more likely source manuscript
2. the direction of flow

3. the secondary manuscript
4. the total number of variation units in which both witnesses are extant

This is followed by a table with columns giving

1. the number of variation units in which the texts of the manuscripts share the same reading
2. the number of variation units in which the reading of Witness 2 is considered secondary to that in Witness 1
3. the number of variation units in which the reading of Witness 1 is considered secondary to that in Witness 2
4. the number of variation units in which no conclusion was reached as to which reading was secondary. (This column is not always included.)

The textual flow between 617 and 2423 is actually somewhat sluggish, more of a fenland river than a mountain stream (see Table 3.1). Under some circumstances we might want to revisit some of these readings in order to make sure that we made good decisions. We may see some other figures which are far more robust. For example, the Initial Text always has all witnesses as descendants, but has no potential ancestors (see Table 3.2).

Sometimes, two manuscripts have an equal give and take between them (see Table 3.3). In the overall textual flow, Gregory-Aland 18

Table 3.1: Comparison of 617 and 2423 in the Letter of James

WITNESSES: 617 → 2423. VARIATION UNITS: 760

Identical	617 → 2423	2423 → 617	Unclear
745	8	5	2

Table 3.2: Comparison of 2423 and the Initial Text in the Letter of James

WITNESSES: INITIAL TEXT → 2423. VARIATION UNITS: 745

Identical	Initial Text → 2423	2423 → Initial Text
669	73	0

Table 3.3: Comparison of 18 and 2423 in the Letter of James

WITNESSES: 18 ↔ 2423. VARIATION UNITS: 760

Identical	18 → 2423	2423 → 18
738	9	9

(Paris, Bibliothèque Nationale Gr. 47) is, like 2423, beneath 617 as a descendant but through another line and with a known intermediary (35 in the diagram).

If we look at the relation of 2423 to the manuscript closest to the critical text selected by the editors, Codex Vaticanus, we can see that the flow from that manuscript is very clear. Even so, there are sixteen passages where the editors consider that the form of text in this thirteenth-century manuscript is older than that in the fourth-century Codex Vaticanus (see Table 3.4).

Table 3.4: Comparison of Codex Vaticanus and 2423 in the Letter of James

WITNESSES: COD. VATICANUS → 2423. VARIATION UNITS: 747

Identical	Cod. Vat. → 2423	2423 → Cod. Vat.
645	70	16

Table 3.5: Comparison of 424 and 2423 in the Letter of James

WITNESSES: 424 → 2423. VARIATION UNITS: 760

Identical	424 → 2423	2423 → 424	Unclear
743	10	6	1

The programme lists all the most likely potential ancestors, and the second most likely ancestor of manuscript 2423 after 617 is 424 (see Table 3.5).[41]

Looking at the data, it has almost as strong a claim to be an ancestor as 617. Why should this not be selected instead of 617? The reason is the way in which the diagram representing the entire textual flow expresses the most likely relationships. Such a calculation, which computes all the possible relationships, has a strength which survives the fairly low differences in flow one way or the other between any two manuscripts and the narrow margins between the likelihoods as to which of two manuscripts is more likely to be the closest ancestor of a third.

Remember that the method sets out to solve the hitherto fatal problem of contamination. We know that it is widespread, but we do not know in any individual place whether it has occurred or not. However, if we simply reconstruct the relationship between the readings (and not the manuscripts) at each place of variation, then each individual reconstruction will hold good regardless of whether the tradition as a whole has suffered contamination. When we put all these results together, then the number of readings which flow in the wrong direction attests the high degree of contamination that has occurred.[42] But it also picks out the readings which are consistent in one direction rather than another, and locates two manuscripts in the tradition on the basis both of that and—a very important point—on the degree of their similarity. This is why the calculation of the degree of agreement between witnesses is so important. It is hard to see how a method which calculated how two manuscripts agreed closely together and showed how they stood in a relationship to the textual flow which fixed their position in a diagram of all witnesses could be a bad guide. And note that even manuscripts at opposite ends of the tradition agree far more than they differ. Thus, one of the manuscripts as far as any along the textual flow from the Initial Text—the Bodleian manuscript Canon. Gr. 34 (Gregory-Aland 522)—still agrees with it in 647 out of 743 passages.[43]

How different this approach is from the traditional generalized theory of text types may be found when we compare Codex Sinaiticus to Codex Vaticanus (see Table 3.6).

To Westcott and Hort these were the two Neutral manuscripts, the leading witnesses in reconstructing the text. Now that we are able to see the figures, 130 years after Westcott and Hort, we find that there is a far lower degree of agreement between them than we found between the Byzantine manuscript 2423 and its relatives. We would expect this: as I said earlier, the survival of a higher proportion of witnesses from the later period means that there are more

Table 3.6: Comparison of codices Vaticanus and Sinaiticus in the Letter of James

WITNESSES: COD. VATICANUS (03) → COD. SINAITICUS (01)
VARIATION UNITS: 747

Identical	03 → 01	01 → 03	Unclear
677	42	18	9

Table 3.7: Five closest potential descendants of Codex Sinaiticus and Codex Vaticanus in the Letter of James

CODEX SINAITICUS (01)

Witness 2	Passages	Identical	01 → Witness 2	Witness 2 → 01
04	469	415	29	21
81	742	650	48	29
307	748	654	52	28
025	711	620	42	36
1735	748	652	51	28

CODEX VATICANUS (03)

Witness 2	Passages	Identical	03 → Witness 2	Witness 2 → 03
04	470	430	29	7
1175	746	677	47	12
01	747	677	42	18
025	712	643	47	13
1243	743	670	49	15

closely related manuscripts. Codex Sinaiticus and Codex Vaticanus disagree seventy times. And here is the surprise: they disagree with each other about as often as 2423, a Byzantine manuscript copied nine hundred years later, differs from the Initial Text! When we look for potential descendants, we find a lower degree of agreement with the most probable candidates (see Table 3.7).

Singular readings

New Testament scholars have sometimes argued that singular readings should be excluded from the calculation of group membership. This is one reason why the theory of text types has been able to survive. Because there are a lot of Byzantine manuscripts, and because most of them are fairly similar, the number of singular readings is not so high. But the oldest manuscripts all have many singular readings, and the reason is that very few of the manuscripts from that period have survived. Take out the singular readings (and these are grammatically possible readings, not accidentals) of the codices Sinaiticus and Vaticanus and they will appear much more similar than they really are. Thus, it is possible to posit an Alexandrian text type. But if we operate with the full figures of the Münster database, then the distance between Westcott and Hort's Neutral manuscripts is as great as that between the text of a thirteenth-century manuscript and the editorial text.

Assessment on the basis of all readings

It is also important to remember that the Münster Method's basic component is the complete transcriptions of the selected witnesses. Once these transcriptions have been compiled into a database, then there are many ways in which it can be used, ways that are not limited to the Münster Method. The complete sets of data allow one to compare manuscripts either by their differences or by the degree of similarity to one another. The old methodology of picking distinctive readings had the weakness that it could not ascertain whether manuscripts simply happened to agree in a few well-known places and overall had a low percentage of agreement. By comparing similarity overall, we are able to deal with another well-known difficulty in traditional stemmatics, namely the possibility—rather, the probability—that a reading may have arisen more than once in the tradition. Certain kinds of common changes, caused by the context or by the natural habits of most copyists, will be misleading evidence for genealogical association. The Münster Method deals with this by observing what it calls the pre-genealogical coherence of witnesses. This consists of a simple percentage of agreement, expressed as 'Witness *x* agrees with witness *y* in *n* out of all cases (or *p* per cent of cases)'. If a variant has arisen twice in the tradition, then the manuscripts attesting the same reading will not necessarily show a high degree of agreement with each other in all readings. The manuscripts of each group will have a high degree of agreement with each other, but not with manuscripts of the other group. Thus simple percentage agreement and disagreement (the degree of pre-genealogical coherence) may be an indicator of a reading having been created more than once.

Evaluation

How well does the method do when we evaluate it against the three requirements I set out at the beginning?

1. The model should be based upon consistent analysis of as complete a collection of data as possible.

There can be no doubt that the method is successful in this respect. Where previous methods have been built upon incomplete sets of data, or on certain striking readings, or on a selection of examples sometimes based on nothing more than a hunch, this has the solid foundation of complete transcriptions, with all differences between the witnesses recorded in a database.

2. The model should be transparent, with all the data and all the process of argument open to the user.

Again, the method scores highly. There is no black box in the Münster Method. No brain can hold the data. A hard drive can. As one eminent scholar said to us at the annual meeting of Studiorum Novi Testamenti Societas, 'A computer is not a New Testament phi-lologist.'[44] Absolutely not, and we're not trying to train it to be one. We are just using it as extra gigabytes in order to supplement our brain power. One does not even have to have a particular textual theory in order to use it. It is better to think of it as a model to expose and interrogate the data, rather than as a set of answers.

3. The model has to be compatible with what we know about the construction of documents, the copying of texts, and the history of the work in question, at each point in its history.

I think that the method is at risk of scoring least highly here, since as it stands we are looking only at texts. For example, we do not know which are the commentary manuscripts. It is true that certain essential bibliographical elements are included. A supplement is treated separately from the main hand of a manuscript. So are corrections. But there is a risk that block mixture may be overlooked. This is the phenomenon where a manuscript is descended from two separate copies, perhaps because an ancestor was damaged and the missing leaves were replaced by copying another exemplar.[45] And in order to substantiate some conclusions with regard to textual affinity, where one is dealing with closely related Byzantine manuscripts, one would want to analyse the physical characteristics as well. A badly written word in the ancestor might show up as a false emendation in its descendant. The reasons for a longer omission might be that it stands as a whole line of text in the ancestor.

This, in brief, is the Münster Method. First used in the edition of the Catholic Epistles as published in *Novum Testamentum Graecum: Editio critica maior*, it is now beginning to be applied in other parts of the New Testament. In time, as it becomes more widely known, it will be adopted by editors of other texts. It continues, and will continue, to be refined and developed. It may be best to continue to think of it as the tool which, by recording the editor's decisions, requires self-criticism, not least because it is an iterative process. What we have learnt about the relationship between manuscripts on the basis of a first round of assessing each variation can then be used to revise the local stemmata, leading to a redefinition of the relationship between manuscripts. We might describe it by para-phrasing Bengel's well-known advice: 'Apply yourself to all the textual evidence; apply all the textual evidence to your theories.'

I have spoken several times about the way in which the written text is only a part of the entire transmission. Scribes will have had mental texts which regularly drove out what was written on the page of their exemplar. Readers will have haphazardly corrected copies to the wording they knew by heart. But the stemmatological method which we have been describing is a tool for describing the relationship between texts. Can it take in its stride the ambient noise of the tradition? I think it can, for two reasons. Let us look again at the textual flow for the catholic letters, and ask what we are looking at. What do the numbers within circles represent? Are they docu-ments? The answer has to be that they are not documents but texts, since the criteria for defining them are purely textual. As it stands, the diagram tells us nothing about the date, characteristics, or his-tory of any of the documents. Once we recognize this, we can make the further observation that there is no need to make a distinction between the written forms of text and the mental texts which were also a strong influence on the transmission of the writings.

The second reason is that the mental forms of the text may be described as another form of contamination, and no different from written corrections taken from other copies. After all, such mental copies are sometimes memories from other written texts, and whether a reading gets into a manuscript from a written correction or a memory, the effect upon the resultant text is the same.

Thus, the method is robust enough to handle the complexities even of the most frequently copied and best-known texts. It is important to remember that it is a method, and its findings are probability rather than absolute truth. Likewise, the diagrams are a representation and not an exact reconstruction. They do not show—of course—how many lost intermediaries there may be. They do not include connections resulting from contamination. They are based on the percentage of flow one way rather than the other. They are designed to represent, and rather like the map of the London Underground they may exaggerate or diminish the distance between items, as we saw with 2423 and 18. But, although it is a method and a way of representing something that in its reality is more complex, what we can say is that the use of databases and the logic required by the method lead towards a high level of consistency. Our goal must be to ensure that its conclusions should be the most accurate which we can at present achieve. Once we have reached as high a degree of consistency as possible, we will have done the best we can with any method. So long as the rules are clear and we keep them, we can be confident that the results will be superior to the alternatives and as good as we can reach at present.

The contribution of the Coherence-Based Genealogical Method to textual scholarship is great. My main question is one of its name.

I find myself wondering whether it is a new method, or the application of a new tool to make an old method—namely Lachmannian stemmatology—work properly. Perhaps it should be called the Coherence-Based Genealogical Application. Setting the technology aside, on what is its claim to be a new method based?

The answer which its developers would give is that it takes pre-genealogical coherence into account.[46] This is simply the number of times manuscripts agree together. That is, it can quantify the frequency of agreement, and make a first common-sense appraisal of manuscript relations based upon this figure, which after all will be far higher than the figures relating to difference. Any two copies of a work will agree more than they differ. If they did not, one would have to conclude that they were not both copies of the same work. This information makes it possible to identify pairs of manuscripts and groups of manuscripts. The group of Gospel manuscripts known as Family 1 was originally identified on the basis of certain distinctive readings. It was then recognized that such readings provided a profile, and the suggestion was made that manuscripts which matched this profile closely enough (the proportion of two-thirds was used) belonged to such a family. The Coherence-Based Genealogical Method makes it possible immediately to identify family members on the basis of the degree of their agreement in all readings.

The development from a methodology which singled out certain indicative readings in order to reconstruct a stemma, to one which uses comparison of witnesses in all the places of variation in order to reconstruct the textual flow, is thus its claim to be a new method. I feel unable to decide on the matter, but on the results I am clear. The presentation of the textual flow showing the relationship between the many states of the text leads us to view the business of New Testament philology in a new light.

In conclusion, the idea of the text as an overall flow is another metaphor for seeing it as a process. The intriguing question with which I will end, and which I will attempt to answer in the next lecture, is: where is the work in the diagram of the textual flow?

Postscript

I gave this lecture in May, and it is several months later. In that time we have come to see that the database which makes the Münster Method work should be more than a way of storing and interrogating textual evidence. Instead, it should be a resource which is interactive with the Virtual Manuscript Room. Then the tools now created within the Workspace for Collaborative Editing (see the next lecture) will form a whole, so that the various kinds of evidence explored in this lecture will no longer be separated from each other, and so that we will also be able to explore physical and historical as well as textual evidence in our quest to understand how the texts of the New Testament works developed and were interpreted.

EDITING THE GREEK
NEW TESTAMENT

man, proud man,
Dress'd in a little brief authority,
Most ignorant of what he's most assur'd

Shakespeare, *Measure for Measure*

Editing the Greek New Testament is the task which has been in the background of everything I have said so far. It is certainly the most complex challenge that faces a New Testament philologist, both technically and theoretically. Moreover, since so few people have the opportunity to undertake the task there is virtually no experience on which to build. The number of editions of the New Testament of any kind is very small. A genuine major critical edition is rarer still. So the edition in which a number of us are currently engaged is a major event.

I finished the third lecture with the question: where is the work in the diagram of the textual flow?

I ask the question again now. Where is the work in the diagram of the textual flow? Is it in the Initial Text? Or is it in all the textual forms throughout the flow (each number represents the text of a manuscript)? The received wisdom is undoubtedly that the work is equivalent to the Initial Text, our name for the editorial text, reconstructed by the scholar on the basis of a thorough analysis of the entire textual tradition. But even if this were so, the work would still exist in a number of forms, since each critical edition has a different Initial Text and therefore presents the work differently. This is particularly true for the New Testament, where views on the quality of an editorial text may be closely connected to a strongly held belief. Of course one thinks here of those people who believe the majority text of the Byzantine world to be divinely inspired and superior to the older manuscripts and to the critical editions. This kind of belief is not something one can engage with at a scholarly level, because it is an a priori view and not one reached by scholarly research. We thus have a situation rare in textual studies as a whole. Few people, so far as I am aware, hold violent and unfounded beliefs with regard to the textual basis of the works of Jane Austen. But with the New Testament, one finds different groups, each with strong views about the content of the work. To one group the Gospel of Mark ends at 16.8, to another at 16.20, and while the latter group will consider the Pericope Adulterae part of John's Gospel, the former will not. These works therefore have a different textual form to different readerships.

It is also noteworthy that for technical reasons, an edition may contain a form of the text that does not represent anything external to the edition. Thus, our edition of the majuscule manuscripts of John contains a text designed to make the apparatus as short as possible.[1] That is, at each point of variation it represents the text of the majority of manuscripts. So it is a text of John, and a useful one, but what is its status? The reading found in the majority of such a selection of manuscripts at any particular place is based upon chance survival. Sometimes the manuscripts split almost fifty-fifty between two readings! This form does not represent the text of any particular, time, place, or stage in the work's textual history. Yet it is a published form of the work.

We must also here acknowledge one of the mysteries of textual scholarship, namely that the Initial Text, the editor's reconstruction of the oldest knowable form, is, from another point of view, the most recent form in existence. Certainly the editor may be allowed to have applied strict logic at every stage of the process, and I am not questioning the results per se. I am only saying that while according to the editor's theory and logic this text must once have existed, for all practical purposes it comes into being on the day that the edition is published. It is striking that we may be sure that the Initial Text was never the text of an actual manuscript, since whatever manuscript once approximated to it will have had its own peculiar errors, which because they were corrected without being reproduced have left no trace behind. Thus the Initial Text has to be regarded as an ideal rather than a real text.

This is an important question to consider, because unless we do so we will be in danger of subscribing to a myth without even knowing that we are doing so. Previously, I quoted the words of B. J. Kemp:

the more I try to make sense of the facts, the more what I write is speculative and begins to merge with the world of historical fiction, a modern form of myth.

We must ask why critical editions are so important a part of the way in which scholars in the humanities go about their business. Is it because they promulgate a very successful myth? Is it because they are so good at hiding the reality of the fact that there is no single authoritative text of a work, that if we were without any edition at all we would be faced by nothing certain but only the multiplicity of forms of text that are present in the manuscripts? The editor is the person who confronts this terrifying anarchy of competing variants, is in effect the scholarly world's exorcist who drives out the legion demons and leaves the work sitting and clothed and in its right mind. There may be an attraction to the editor in wielding such power. There may be relief to everyone else, a sense that the world is a safer place once the text has been reduced to order, the competing forms fragmented into a critical apparatus. But is the multiplicity of texts really a terrifying and destructive force that must be controlled? Perhaps it is rather a richness which could never be attained by a single form of the text, so that the tradition as a whole contains a greater wisdom. If so, does the critical edition have to be a tool for turning chaos into order? Are there other ways of understanding its role? The answers to these questions will emerge in the course of the lecture.

The beginning of the way to an answer is found through the observation which I made with regard to understanding how manuscripts are related, that the undertaking is an attempt to create a narrative. Bear in mind the idea of a narrative. A critical edition is above all an attempt to make sense of the facts. A good critical edition may be so good that we will not even realize it to be that attempt and treat it as the work itself *tout simple*. It may be so persuasive that it will be accepted as the only true form of the work, perhaps for generations. But I hope that what I have had to say so far will have convinced you that one should not attribute so much weight to any one form of the works composing the New Testament. Personally I believe that there are good reasons why we should regard the work as including all the forms of text that we find in the manuscripts. I am not saying that in historical terms all the forms are equivalent. Rather, I draw attention to their importance as the forms in which the work was known and copied throughout its development. Some came into being later than others, and would never be taken as contenders to be the Initial Text. But they are still a part of the entire tradition as we know it, and have their part to play in our memory of what it is. One may go further and say that the work is found in all the forms, handwritten, printed, digital, and remembered, in which the work has ever been made or repeated.

The first thing therefore to be said about a critical edition is not that it *is* the work, but that it is a description of the work in its different forms. It is a tool for understanding the work. How does it do this? What does it contain?

The components of a critical edition

What criteria does an edition have to fill to be regarded as critical? Is it true that the Society of Biblical Literature's Greek New Testament, published in 2010, is a critical edition, as it claims to be?[2] It has a critical text, contains no apparatus except a statement of the readings of other editions and one English translation, and has no explanation of its editorial choices.

Is the edition of Westcott and Hort a critical edition? It has a critical text and a few alternative readings in the margins but contains no apparatus.[3] It has a generalized explanation of its editorial choices in a volume of introduction.

Is Tischendorf's *Editio octava critica maior* a critical edition?[4] It has a large apparatus, a critical text but no explanation of its editorial choices.

At the most demanding level, I believe that we still await a truly critical edition of the New Testament. One might divide the past editions into two classes: those which made an important contribution to improving the critical text, and those which brought together a critical apparatus which set out the important data as it was known at the time. To the former class belong the editions of Lachmann, Tregelles, and Westcott and Hort.[5] To the latter belong those of Mill (1707), Matthaei (1782–88), and Tischendorf.[6] A proper critical edition must combine the two. It must contain a scientifically constructed critical text, and a critical apparatus which provides the supporting evidence. This is universally agreed. But I have come to believe that it must also contain a third component, the editors' justification for their decisions at each point of variation. No editor in the past has done this except in general terms (as, for example, Westcott and Hort did in their introduction). Such an edition is now possible, and I believe that the *Editio critica maior* will achieve it. I am not claiming infallibility for its decisions, but only pointing out that it has the structure and means necessary for it to be truly critical in combining these three elements. The edition of the text is accompanied by a volume of editorial commentary. From the edition of John onwards, the material in this explanatory volume will be generated by a comments section in the interface for making the edition, which I will describe later.

In this respect it already marks a significant step forward. In other ways it is not only significant, it is also long overdue. This becomes clear when we consider the following.

How the previous critical editions became outdated

The three major editions of the second half of the nineteenth century were by Tregelles (1857–79), Tischendorf (1869–72), and Westcott and Hort (1881). They appeared in the quarter of a century between 1857 and 1881. The situation of scholarship in that period was one of exploration. Lachmann's methodological work was so recent that it cannot have been fully absorbed, except in so far as it offered a system for replacing the Textus Receptus, which had held sway since the sixteenth century. Certainly, scholars had been aware of the shortcomings of the Textus Receptus since the end of the seventeenth century, but nobody until Lachmann had produced a convincing alternative. It is even more telling though that the materials which were most important to these editors, certainly to Tischendorf and Hort, were only beginning to be studied. The New Testament of Codex Sinaiticus had come to the attention of Western scholars very recently, in Tischendorf's facsimile of 1862—and therefore when Tregelles' work was well under way (the Gospels had already been published). Twenty years is not long enough to form a proper understanding of a new find of this significance. It is not so widely appreciated that it was also only in the 1860s that a complete and careful transcription of Codex Vaticanus became available to scholarship. So while scholars realized that in these two manuscripts they had a resource for gaining a better understanding of the fourth-century text, they did not yet have the detailed knowledge of the materials. Nor did they possess the experience to make full use of it. It is easy to say, over a century later, that Tischendorf followed the readings of Codex Sinaiticus too frequently and that Hort had too great a faith in the Vaticanus. But one should not be surprised. They were trying their hardest to incorporate this fresh evidence. It is arguable that scholars today have still not fully absorbed the new evidence provided by the Bodmer papyri, and they have been known for fifty years. It would be unfair to criticize the great nineteenth-century editors for not having a full understanding of materials that had been known for less than half that time. It is important therefore in evaluating the work of those editors that we take full account of the fact that they were pioneers taking the first steps towards critical editions, whose first concern was to provide something better than the Textus Receptus. The greatest mistake that has been made may have been to regard their work as the completion of a process, rather than the beginning of a new era.[7]

The codices Sinaiticus and Vaticanus alone required thorough study, not least a thorough comparison with each other, which should have necessitated a successor to the existing editions in the early twentieth century. But it never happened. Increasingly, the text of Westcott and Hort was regarded as the apotheosis of the critical edition. But if we consider the twentieth century as well, it is marked by the discovery at regular intervals of papyri whose texts turned everything people thought they knew upside down. These papyri contained forms of text from the third and perhaps even the late second centuries. Apart from the light that they shed on the book as an artefact, they put the nineteenth-century editions right out of date. The three Chester Beatty papyri, between them comprising some part of most of the books of the New Testament, were published in the 1930s.[8] The Bodmer papyri came in the late 1950s and early 1960s.[9] There has been a steady stream of Oxyrhynchus papyri since 1898 and already in the present century we are trying to assimilate important new witnesses to the Apocalypse and the Acts of the Apostles.[10] Each new discovery made the old critical apparatuses ever more out of date, and, even more worryingly, cast doubt on the quality of existing critical texts.

It is also important to note that the twentieth century saw a growth in the number of Byzantine manuscripts known to scholarship through the development of systematic lists. Gregory's catalogue of 1908 listed 4,012 manuscripts and the number today has risen by another 1,600. In this period, as a result of more accurate lists, the number to have been carefully examined has also risen.

Many of the most significant manuscripts, such as the two copied by Ephraim which I mentioned in my third lecture, have come to light as a result of these studies, and the discovery of the survival of ancient forms of text in comparatively late manuscripts has cast new light on the history of the Byzantine text. This has led to a reappraisal of the textual history of the New Testament works. Within the Byzantine text (as the evidence of the previous lecture bears out), we know far more than we did about many of the families and groups of manuscripts.

But in spite of the fact that the twentieth century saw research of many kinds, much of it of the highest quality, the frequent absence of critical editions in progress meant that the research had no impact on the text, either in Greek or in modern translations, and thus on scholarly and general interpretation of the text. Most scholarship consisted of essays and monographs on particular problems and readings, and a good deal of fulmination about the shortcomings of the editions.

A major critical edition at last offers the opportunity to bring all this research to bear on a single purpose.

Finally, the advances in computer tools for editing and the consequent advances in studying textual variation require us to make a new critical edition.

I have painted quite a gloomy picture, of technically imperfect editions that are a century and more out of date. You may ask how we have been able to get by. Where has one had to go for textual evidence? How do we know the wording of the manuscripts, if Westcott and Hort have no apparatus and that of Tischendorf is so old that it lacks many of the most significant manuscripts? Back in the seventies it was a real struggle, because we did not have an edition whose apparatus systematically included all of the manuscripts people were most interested in, namely the Chester Beatty and Bodmer papyri, some important majuscules such as the Freer Gospels, and minuscules—notably Ephraim's two manuscripts. One had to work with a couple of older editions (certainly Tischendorf, who provides information lacking anywhere else, and possibly von Soden if one could trust him) and the plates or *editiones principes* of the papyri. Starting out at that point, one had to get hold of those nineteenth-century editions and at least half a dozen facsimile editions.

If one was not a philologist but had a different interest in the New Testament writings, one relied on a hand edition. Such a convenient copy, designed for use by others—scholars, students, clergy—should consist of a critical text and a succinct apparatus.

Unfortunately, the situation was not that much better for many decades so far as hand editions went either. The popular edition of the twentieth century was the Nestle, based upon the consensus of late nineteenth-century editions and with a minimal apparatus. If you compare it with Tischendorf you see how little information there is about textual variation. Limited and misleading though it was, this edition went through twenty-five editions and reigned more or less unchallenged from 1898 to 1966. Other editions which were widely used in the English-speaking world were similarly limited. The British and Foreign Bible Society's 1904 edition was a slight revision of Nestle. Alexander Souter's 1910 edition was an adaptation of the Textus Receptus to show the text implied by the Revised Version of 1881, with a tiny apparatus.

Looking to continental Europe, the editions of Merk (1933) and Bover (1943) both suffered from idiosyncratic views and had an apparatus that was either unreliable (Merk) or very small (Bover).[11] What was needed was a properly constructed text and a consistent apparatus suitable for a hand edition, which would include the new manuscript finds of the century. The first step was the appearance in 1966 of the first edition of the United Bible Societies' *Greek New Testament*.[12] It contained a rather full apparatus for 1,440 variant readings and a text selected by a group of leading scholars. One should not underestimate, either, the importance of the beautifully legible typeface, which showed up the crabbed and archaic appearance of all its competitors. The companion volume of textual commentary gives an explanation of the committee's judgements, though it is not clear how far this was written in retrospect rather than as a contemporary record. The *Greek New Testament* has gone through several editions, the fifth published in 2012, and the sixth now in the first stages of preparation.

The next step was the publication of the Nestle-Aland edition in 1979. This contained the same text as the United Bible Societies' edition, with an apparatus that included all the important readings of the papyri and majuscules and a significant number of minuscules, along with versional evidence and patristic citations. A revised edition appeared in 1993. The apparatus is regularly updated with fresh evidence and corrections. Further revisions of text and apparatus, in tandem with the *Greek New Testament* edition, are planned as the Nestle-Aland edition continues to be published.

Of course, this is the wrong way around. One would expect a hand edition to provide a digest of a major critical edition. The Nestle-Aland edition is a fine tool, and one could not imagine being without it. But it is a stopgap, awaiting the completion of the *Editio critica maior*. The text is not the result of a study of all the evidence, since it pre-dates the development of the Münster Method and the other computer tools now available, and the witnesses are not selected on the basis of the analysis of all witnesses in test passages. Nestle-Aland continues to be an essential tool, not least for getting one's bearings in the first stages of preparing a critical edition. But it will be replaced in 2032 by a new hand edition which will contain a systematic digest of the *Editio critica maior*.

It is thus arguable that the *Editio critica maior* is the first critical edition to be based upon these necessary steps:

1. a systematic assessment of all witnesses to the text in order to select those which are most important and which illustrate the textual history
2. a mature consideration of those witnesses, using a consistent methodology which analyses full sets of data with the means to carry out the complicated calculations necessary to establish the relationships between the manuscripts
3. a reconstruction of the oldest form of text recoverable by that analysis
4. a complete and systematic apparatus
5. a full explanation and justification of its methodology and conclusions.

So far only the Catholic Epistles have appeared. Work on Acts is nearing completion, John is not far behind, and Mark is in hand. Paul is beginning in Birmingham and work on the Apocalypse has started in Wuppertal.

While the processes of making a critical edition may seem to be of interest only to editors, I believe that all users of the New Testament need to know enough of them to understand what it is that they hold in their hands, whether they are reading a translation or studying the Greek text. So what I am going to do is to describe the process of the *Editio critica maior* from the conception of the idea to its delivery. If it is true that critical editions are central to the practice of textual scholarship, then this explanation will also show how everything I have spoken about in these lectures hitherto is coherent.

The *Editio critica maior* was originally conceived by Kurt Aland, the founder of the Institute for New Testament Textual Research in Münster-in-Westphalia. Aland's conception and groundwork were generally impeccable.[13] The last twenty years of technological development have made it possible to realize the concept in a more thoroughgoing way than he could have imagined. Described as 'the textual history of the first millennium', the edition sets out to present the entire known textual history of the New Testament through an apparatus containing all the variant readings of selected manuscripts. The first step was to list the witnesses. As I observed at the beginning of my second lecture, they divide into three categories:

Greek manuscripts
citations in early Christian writers in Greek
translations into other languages, which comprise both manuscripts
    and citations.

I will deal with each in turn.

Greek manuscripts

The initial requirement was to make a list of all known manuscripts. The second was to acquire microfilm of every manuscript. This was achieved to a high degree of success, sometimes through buying them and where necessary by means of a famed series of expeditions to Greek monasteries by a Münster team armed with the necessary equipment. Once this was done, the next stage was to choose the most appropriate manuscripts to be included. They have been selected through a screening process which consisted of collecting the reading of every accessible manuscript at a set of test passages in every book of the New Testament.[14] The number of test passages has varied, as have some of the details of the analysis. In the case of the Gospel of John, this system has been augmented by an even more ambitious project, the collecting of every variant reading of all the accessible manuscripts in the whole of Chapter 18. The end result provides about 400 significant variation units in the forty verses of the chapter. So with these systems of test passages we have complete sets of data. By compiling this information electronically and storing it in a database, with specially created editing tools, we are able to assess the relationship between all the texts in a way which has never before been possible. These are the tools which I described in the third lecture.[15] We begin to see that, great as the achievements of previous editors were, they were working with partial and arbitrarily selected materials which led to theories of the text and its history which were themselves partial, and thus almost bound to be mistaken. Once one is able to collect full sets of data consistently, the way is at last open to select manuscripts to be included according to a consistent set of criteria, which may even be used to ensure that as many variant readings are included in as few witnesses as possible.[16]

Once the witnesses have been selected, they are transcribed in full electronically, according to standard conventions which are compliant with the Text Encoding Initiative.[17] This ensures longevity and means that they may be used by other groups. A transcription can be made in one of two ways: by typing the whole text from the manuscript, or by taking a base text and altering it at each point of difference to conform to the text of the manuscript. The latter is more practical. Each witness is transcribed twice, and the two transcriptions are compared and all disagreements resolved and corrected in one of the copies. This final copy is then exported into XML, and published in the Institutional Repository under a Creative

Commons licence, so that anybody can use it. Part of the purpose of the electronic transcription is that it will not become obsolete. This will relieve one of the biggest curses of textual editing, the need to do the work over again for every edition. Thus already we have produced transcriptions of Codex Sinaiticus which have been used on four different websites, each in a different format.[18] Another benefit of the electronic transcription is that it can be improved where error is spotted, in a process which minimizes the risk of a fresh error creeping in.

Finally, as I emphasized in the third lecture, the transcriptions are all placed in a database and collated with each other. This provides a complete set of data which can be edited and analysed according to the Münster Method, or for that matter according to any existing theory or further development. It also provides the user with the complete set of raw data by which to assess the edition itself.

Time and again one comes up with questions of workflow in making an edition. The essence of workflow is not time but sequence and above all transition. As textual scholars we know that error occurs in a work where it passes from one place to another. In the pre-print world of manuscripts, that transition was when a codex was copied to make a new one. In the print age, it occurs at the stage of typesetting. The workflow of a critical edition in the digital age should be designed to reduce the points of transition to a minimum. This is a primary concern in another project, which is developing a Workspace for Collaborative Editing, with partners in Birmingham, Münster, and Trier.[19] The critical transition is the making of the transcription, when the material crosses from the manuscript to the digital medium. Ideally, this should be the only transition. Thereafter, the corrected material should not be altered. Only the way in which it is presented should be managed. This is done in several ways:

1. The 'noise' (what is known to bibliographers as the accidentals) of spelling errors and *lapsus calami* must be eliminated. But this is done without touching the transcription. All that is done is to use a feature which treats the orthographic variation as equivalent to the 'standard' spelling chosen for the edition.
2. Where many manuscripts are compared, the extent of each variation unit has to be controlled by the editor. This again controls the presentation but not the raw data.

There should be no manual keying in of data after the initial stage of collecting.

At this point the apparatus exists as a set of variants to the Nestle-Aland text, which is used as a starting-point for the new critical text. It is in a database with an interface which allows the editor to study it and recover data.

Patristic citations

Traditionally listed in a card index, the citations are today recorded in a database. Again the critical step is transferring data from the cards or the editions into the database. As our tools develop, we will increasingly be drawing on existing databases available on the internet, and in turn contributing to them. What sort of data do we want to record? Of course, the text of the citation, the author, work, and reference. Also, material to allow us to make proper use of the citation. Is it a careful quote, an adaptation, an allusion? What is the introductory formula? Is it part of a longer quotation or chain of quotations? Are there variant readings in the manuscript tradition of the writing? Are there any habits of citation by the author which may affect the wording? It is little use to record a citation without adding this other information, because the evidence has every time to be weighed. And how far can we trust the edition of the writer on which we draw? There are no critical editions of many writings, and we are too often dependent on Migne's Patrologia Graeca, which usually simplifies earlier editions such as those by the Benedictines of St Maur. Even where we now have a more recent edition, it may not be a critical edition, or it may be a bad critical edition. Editors often make extraordinary decisions with regard to the biblical text which they print. They may supply lemmata to a commentary where they are absent in the manuscripts, or they may standardize the biblical text to a modern edition. Unless one goes to the manuscripts, such corruptions of the text may pass unnoticed.[20]

In spite of these problems, we need to record the reliable evidence. Once the database of citations has been made, the editors will compare the data with the evidence of the manuscripts, and add it to the apparatus when it is appropriate to do so.

Versions

Each of the ancient versions is of great interest in its own right. In the case of the oldest forms of the Latin, Syriac, and Coptic, the manuscripts are as old as any of the parchment manuscripts in Greek, and the date at which the translation was made pre-dated them. Where two versions agree, they provide evidence for a form of Greek text older than the making of either translation, and this may provide very valuable evidence which reveals information about forms of the text known in the second century. But their use in a critical edition of the Greek needs, as the citations do, to be handled carefully. The influence of the language into which a version has been translated must be considered for many kinds of variants. So even if the version shows a variation which is present in Greek manuscripts, it will be necessary to consider whether or not it may have arisen within the version and therefore be inadmissible evidence. It is also possible that a variant may have arisen independently in the version, just as we saw it may do within the Greek tradition.

The only way to attempt to resolve such problems is by making a separate edition of the version. The history of the *Editio critica maior* and the research interests of the Münster Institute and the International Greek New Testament Project (IGNTP) are both paralleled by a series of tools for versional research. Thus along with the *Editio critica maior* of John stand editions (both print and electronic) of the Latin, Coptic, Syriac, and Gothic versions.

Once this is done, each versional editor will add their data to the database behind the critical edition of the Greek. The Greek patristic citations will also need to be added. This will be achieved by using an interface tailored to each user which will show them the variant readings in the Greek witnesses and enable them to add their own witnesses or, where necessary, a new variant. This stage is designed so that again there is no disruptive transition. The Greek citations will be linked into the main database of readings, so that no typing is required. Editors of versions will be able to enter text in the language of the version, again by importing text rather than by typing it.

Once all the versional and citational information has been added, those preparing the Greek edition will be able to complete the task of selecting the critical text. This will be done using the Münster Method, which I have already described. One important feature of the editorial tool is that it provides a field for recording the justification for each decision made, so that it will not be possible to move on from that variant until a justification has been given.

The options of the digital edition are very valuable in another respect. Where there is so much data, old editors were faced with a formidable task every time they wanted to change their base text. Since all variant readings are expressed as variation from the base text, it followed that every time the base text was changed the editor needed to correct the apparatus. This process is both time-consuming and extremely prone to error. The result has been a strong inbuilt conservatism since editions became large. When in 1926 a committee was formed in Britain to make a new critical edition, it was quickly decided instead to make a new apparatus, using the text of Westcott and Hort.[21] In the case of this edition's successor, the International Greek New Testament Project, it resulted in the decision to produce an edition of Luke which consisted solely of a large critical apparatus to the Textus Receptus.[22] In the editorial milieu of the database, this is no longer a problem, since the database will recalibrate the apparatus on the basis of a new base text. It will do so using the concept of a baseless apparatus.[23] This is valuable for other reasons, as I shall show in the next lecture.

Then follows the output. This may be in two formats: in the traditional print edition, and as an online edition. The latter will certainly provide access to the raw data—transcriptions, citations, and the versions. It will also include analytical tools and search facilities, which will allow the user to replicate the editors' decisions or to try out their own and observe the consequences.

The value of the Editio critica maior

I asked the question, why do we need a critical edition? In order to answer it, we must consider a wider set of questions with regard to its value. What does it do in the world of textual scholarship? I would like to draw your attention to four important functions which it serves.

First of all, the process itself is essential for the impetus it gives to textual scholarship and palaeography as a whole. The development of methodologies and analytical tools, the discussions surrounding particular problems, questions about the status and quality of the editorial texts available, the opportunities for research and employment, all these mean that every generation needs critical editions for the good of all the disciplines associated with a particular work. Not least important in this regard is the fact that it is too big a task for individuals, and has therefore to be carried out by teams. The *Editio critica maior* has separate groups working in Münster, Wuppertal, and Birmingham. The last named of these groups, which also doubles as the IGNTP, consists of many people, including a funded core team and volunteer contributors from within and beyond academia. Well over one hundred people are participating at any one time.

Without such an international partnership, textual criticism would consist of individuals and small local concentrations of researchers pursuing their own interests. Such a large project requires opportunities for new people to be trained in reading and transcribing manuscripts and in other relevant skills.[24]

Secondly, the opportunity to be an editor of the Greek New Testament is an exciting challenge, which very few have the opportunity to undertake. It requires a range of scholarly skills, including the command of a range of broad facts and details and the ability to make consistent decisions. But a successful edition also requires wider skills: the ability to work within a diverse team is one. Another is organization. The fact is that probably the most important requirement for a complex critical edition is good organization. If the practices are not clearly laid down and followed, if the workflow is not precise, if data is not gathered carefully and stored safely, then however good the research, the edition will be a bad one. I strongly suspect that the faults in von Soden's edition lie not in the scholarship but in planning and then in carrying out the project. A successful critical edition therefore requires careful organization and execution by a team of people who are able to work well together. It is stating the obvious to say that discord within a team may harm the edition. Clear roles for everyone involved, and a way of discussing and resolving differences are essential. I mention these matters because I want to stress how much a critical edition is part of the whole fabric of scholarship and teaching. It does not happen somewhere else, but like the rest of what we do is a complex enterprise involving people and ideas, institutions, relationships, and the unexpected.

Thirdly, a critical edition is important for the further uses of the text that will be created. All students studying the New Testament in Greek, from first-year undergraduate level up, all New Testament scholars including exegetes and historians, as well as educators and researchers worldwide, use one or other of the two hand editions I mentioned earlier, either the United Bible Societies' *The Greek New Testament* or the Nestle-Aland *Novum Testamentum Graece*. The text of these editions will come to be based upon the critical text and apparatus of the *Editio critica maior*. Since there will be no replacement for at least a generation (perhaps even the 150 years that the 1869 edition by Tischendorf has survived), one may estimate that the *Editio critica maior* will be around for quite a while after its completion twenty years from now.

It is not only the Greek New Testament that will be affected. Since the United Bible Societies and Nestle-Aland editions are the basis of almost all the translations of the New Testament, all vernacular Bibles will also depend on the text of the *Editio critica maior*.

Thus the eventual influence of a critical edition will far exceed the number of people who actually use it. In terms of methodology, the work may be expected to influence editors of other texts, and thus to have an impact across a range of textual traditions, be the texts sacred or not.

Fourthly, in the current digital revolution, the development of new methodologies and tools is essential. The *Editio critica maior* is playing a leading role in attracting and harnessing the resources needed to make aspirations into realities. The electronic and web-based editions and tools which it has inspired are at least as important as the print outputs. I will say more about this in the next lecture, when I describe what the New Testament is becoming.

I have described the *Editio critica maior*, and critical editions in general, and I have touched several times on the importance of knowing what it is and what it is not. Let me now set out the key elements in a definition of a true critical edition of the New Testament.

1. A critical edition is not a reconstruction of an authorial text. It is a reconstruction of the oldest recoverable text, the Initial Text. We discussed the authorial fallacy in the first lecture. I have showed also how the Initial Text is the text which can be reconstructed as necessarily lying behind the extant witnesses. The question of the gap between that Initial Text and older forms is not, I argued, a question which should concern us here. I say again that the user who treats the text of James in the *Editio critica maior* as identical to a letter written several hundred years before the oldest extant manuscript was copied has made a serious methodological error.

2. A critical edition claims neither completeness nor infallibility. It does seek accuracy and consistency. I have said already of the Coherence-Based Genealogical Method that it is not absolute truth, but a method with a set of rules to be followed consistently.

The same is true of the *Editio critica maior*. As Klaus Wachtel has said, it is the *Editio maior* not the *Editio maxima*. It will not tell us everything, but it has to be trustworthy in what it does tell us.

3. A critical edition has to be transparent, it has to set out for the user all the evidence so that it can be scrutinized and corrected. Like the Münster Method, it must contain no black box, but must expose both the methodology and the raw data so that anybody can see, test, and improve what it has done.

4. It is more than a store of data. The subtitle of the *Editio critica maior* is 'The textual history of the first millennium'. It therefore contains a narrative structure. In fact it tells the story of a process, namely of the text's development. Perhaps a page of critical apparatus does not seem what one might expect a story to be like, but for those prepared to read and to learn, that is precisely what it is. This is the most important point I have to make. The text cannot be read apart from the apparatus. In fact, from the purely technical point of view, the text exists only as a series of hooks on which the apparatus hangs. If we revisit the *Editio critica maior*, we will see that the text has every word and space numbered. Each variant is expressed with a lower case letter related to those numbers. Without the text, there could be no apparatus. At the same time, it is also true that without the apparatus there could be no text, since the text is determined by a study of the variant readings and thus is a logical consequence of the observation of the variants.

In short, the critical edition is the most advanced tool we have for making the New Testament, and for describing it—and here I use the word 'describing' in a positive way. In itself and in the further uses of hand editions and translations to which it is put, it is a potent and highly influential way of making the New Testament. It permeates cultural attitudes to the Bible, in a way that is out of all proportion to the number of people likely to use it.

I suggested at the beginning that part of the success of the critical edition in Western scholarship may be that it seems to foster the myth of an authoritative and definitive single version of the work, in which all the other versions in which it once existed are reduced to a set of footnotes. But it does not have to foster this myth. It only does so for the lazy person who decides to ignore the critical appa-ratus. Take it as a whole, text and apparatus together, and it refuses to give credence to the idea that there is a single definitive version of the text. Instead, each variant is a narrative about the history of the text: the line of text at the top tells us how the story begins, the apparatus about how it continued. What the line at the top does not tell us is how the story ends, because the story continues with each reading of the text and apparatus. There is no definitive version of the work.

I will close by repeating that we have the technology to build on existing editions instead of starting afresh each time. Because of this, the *Editio critica maior* has the potential to be different from every edi-tion that has gone before. Moreover, a digital edition need never be finished, but can instead be an ever-improving tool for studying the New Testament text. The *Editio critica maior* is therefore not the com-pletion of an era in scholarship, but the beginning of a new one.

THE NEW TESTAMENT
OF THE FUTURE

Journeys end in lovers tweeting....
What's to come is still unsure.

(with apologies to William Shakespeare)

The New Testament of the future is likely to be very different from anything made hitherto. This is for one simple reason: textual scholarship today is passing through one of the greatest revolutions since the first texts were written. The new world offered by the computer has already had at least as profound an effect on what we do as did the introduction of printing half a millennium ago. And like pioneers such as Gutenberg, our work is only a beginning. We can look back now at the first printed editions of the New Testament and see how much they were like manuscripts. As time went by, technology and scholarship developed hand in hand. Nobody could mistake the Complutensian Polyglot, printed sixty years after Gutenberg, for a manuscript. In fifty years, our current achievements will certainly seem valiant but quaint, since we have discovered a whole new technology and yet insist on treating the computer screen as though it were a page in a codex or, even worse, a roll. So our technological advances have also taken us back two thousand years as though the codex had never existed. Somewhere just over the horizon lies something quite different. Unfortunately I cannot impress you with my foresight, since I have no idea what that something is. The best I can do is to describe what we are doing and what we are starting to do, and how this will change the New Testament. I invite you to keep in mind some of the key themes which have been present throughout these lectures. In particular, I observed in my fourth lecture that the critical edition is the most advanced tool we have for describing the New Testament. I was using the word 'describing' in a positive way, but as it stands the printed critical edition has the weakness that it is so different from the manuscripts and feels so divorced from them. Of course, if we revisit the concept of 'making the New Testament', we may say that just as the various formats through which the works passed, such as codex and printed book, were each accompanied by its own concept of the nature of the New Testament, so we cannot expect the New Testament made by the critical edition to be necessarily like each former manuscript existence. Nevertheless, inasmuch as philology is a historical discipline, it is desirable that the historical formats of the works should be considered. The current format of the critical edition makes it hard to locate the textual evidence within the manuscripts. In my ideal world, we need a way of bringing the critical edition and the manuscripts *as* manuscripts back together again. We will then have the best of both worlds, one in which we can study the tradition as a whole at the same time as exploring the actual forms in which it was present at each point.

The edition of the future will also find new ways of presenting the edition as a narrative. This is neatly illustrated by a publisher's blurb I saw for an electronic English Bible: 'An ebook 2000 years in the making.' It's a slogan that highlights the history of the works as a process. The idea that the ebook is somehow the apotheosis of the

Bible is a daring claim, on a par with the claim by the Elzevir brothers in 1633 that their text of the New Testament was received by everybody everywhere.[1] But we must not assume that the ebook is the final word. Who knows in what further formats the Bible will be published in the future?

Our tools

We use tools to make something. To start with we may need to make tools in order to make other tools. Or to put it differently, we make tools for ourselves and then we make things which work for other people. At the invention of printing, Gutenberg needed to develop tools to make the matrix in which the type was cast. Counterpunches and letter punches had to be designed and made for every letter or glyph, making up a complete font. Digital editing is in a similar situation. Most of the time, we are working out how to use the medium for ourselves, and the time spent making materials available to other people can easily come in second place, even though it is the easier part. For example, the greater challenge lies in creating the database we need to collect and analyse the material. Building an interface to allow everyone easy access to it is simple. If we consider the Münster Method, which I discussed in the third lecture, it has been under development since the early nineties. But only now are the tools being developed which will make it usable by everyone. So although we have been using computers for twenty years, we are only beginning to see the impact of computer technology on the entire research environment for the humanities. These tools are most significant not in their immediate purpose but in the way that they change the relationship between the user and the textual data. I hope to demonstrate this in the next few paragraphs.

For the student of a text, the focus of research is textual data. In the traditional format, this data has been mediated to us via critical editions (or sometimes uncritical editions). If you want to study the Greek New Testament, you use your Nestle-Aland, and thank heaven that Dr Nestle and Professor Aland are there to help you, because systematically accessing the documentary data at first hand would be virtually impossible. By and large you trust them blindly—for accuracy, and for their editorial decisions. But I hope that I have shown that this is not what a critical edition should be for. If it is indeed, as I have argued, a narrative of the history of the text, then we can readily imagine that the traditional print version is not the only medium and maybe not the best medium for telling the story. Online editions are providing us with new media which will give users a different and in some ways a better understanding of the work and the edition. I have already discussed some of these tools. Most notably, I have discussed online databases listing the manuscripts and other materials, and the suite which makes up the Coherence-Based Genealogical Method. But the most important tool of all consists of making available to the user the primary material out of which the edition has been made: the manuscripts.

Mass digitization

There is nothing to beat the experience of going into a library and examining a manuscript in the flesh. But the experience does have its difficulties. It involves travel, possibly a long way, and therefore can be expensive. It takes time, and has to be fitted into the library's schedule. Nevertheless, for some kinds of research it remains essential. If one is studying the details of a manuscript's composition, or needs to read things which the photographer's art has failed to reproduce, or sometimes simply for ease of consultation in turning the pages, there is no replacement for autopsy. Even so, one would rather be able to do it at home (as scholars often did until modern times when librarians became more protective of their irreplaceable artefacts than they were even in the days of M. R. James). If you were able to consult all the manuscripts of your work at home, would not this be much easier? Today it is possible, if you have high quality images available. And what is even more extraordinary, such images may be easier to read than the manuscript itself.

The most important event in humanities research today is what we call mass digitization. Let us think back a moment to the time before computers and before cameras, say between the late seventeenth century and the middle of the nineteenth. A few scholars visited libraries, examined manuscripts, and wrote down from them what they could: descriptions and a list of their variant readings. Sometimes such a scholar would make a complete transcription of a manuscript. The only way in which that information could become available to people who had not seen the manuscript was through a critical edition in which its readings were reported, or through a printed transcription. The critical edition served as a repository for all such information. This situation changed with the invention of photography. It then became possible to publish a facsimile of a manuscript, which gave someone who had not seen it a great deal more information about its appearance and the text it contained. The more sophisticated facsimiles even included a transcription as well. The drawback with this technology was that because it remained expensive, the benefits were felt by only a few people, namely those with enough money or enthusiasm to buy their own copy, or those with access to a large research library.

Mass digitization, which is rapidly expanding at an institutional and national level, consists of the online publication of digital images of the primary data of humanities research. It transforms the situation totally. One of the most significant such programmes in the UK for the New Testament is the digitizing of all its Greek manuscripts by the British Library.[2] There are even national projects.[3]

The next stage after such institutional collections is logical collections, in which images of all the manuscripts of a particular work are drawn into a single place. We can see this approach via our own website, the Virtual Manuscript Room.[4] One part, hosting material referring to the Mingana Collection, is an institutional collection. Another part, which is developed by our colleagues in the Münster Institute, is a logical collection dealing with Greek New Testament manuscripts.

There are pros and cons to the logical collection. It will benefit from the expertise of researchers thoroughly familiar with a work and its bibliography. On the other hand, it may create a false definition. Having argued in the second lecture that there is no such thing as a New Testament manuscript, I do not want to fall into the trap of supposing that a logical collection containing only images of so-called New Testament manuscripts, or of those pages of composite manuscripts containing New Testament works, is necessarily desirable. Just as I suggested that the best way to catalogue the manuscripts of a particular work is by first making a catalogue of all manuscripts, so I suggest that the best way to build logical collections of images is by first digitizing all manuscripts. This is best attained by the institutional collections, which will go through an entire library imaging everything. Once that is done, scholars interested in a particular work, such as the Gospel of John, will be able to harvest images of it. Such a process has other advantages: the efficiency of developing institutional collections will always be greater. At the same time, there is a place for groups with specialist interests. In the past both the Münster Institute and the International Greek New Testament Project played an important role in microfilming manuscripts. Today the Center for the Study of New Testament Manuscripts in Plano, Texas, has raised private funds and made images of a number of manuscripts, often in libraries without the facilities to do their own digitizing or in private collections.[5] The biggest hope for a dramatic increase in the images available, however, lies with mass digitization in major libraries.

It is also worth pointing out that logical collections need not, and should not, consist of materials duplicated on the research group's own server. It should consist of links to the material on other servers. This is one of the functions of the Virtual Manuscript Room, for which the ontology of documents, texts, and work has been developed so that a user may harvest all the material relating to a particular work or part of a work from across the web.

Images are the most important thing for the present and in the immediate future. You do not even need to know Greek to appreciate the beauty of a manuscript. They are easier to understand than any transcription or edition will ever be. The most important requirement in New Testament research, and in the study of all other written works, is to have high-resolution digital colour images of the documents. The only frustrating aspect of writing these lectures has been the difficulty of illustrating them. Either I could find no images of a manuscript, or I could only find a digitization of a black-and-white microfilm.

But mass digitization is not primarily about scholarly convenience. I suggested in the first lecture that we don't have to use critical editions. In fact we could today dispense with printed texts altogether and instead read the works of the New Testament in images of the manuscripts. If we were to do this, we would need ways of finding and connecting the different copies. And the more images of the more documents we have, and with that the more texts, the more we would need to anchor the work in this wealth of material. It follows that from the images I need two things:

- a description and indexing system which tells me what each document is like physically on each page and where all the text, paratext, and miniatures may be found, all in a database;
- a transcription.

The description, indexing, transcription, and images of a manuscript locate the textual findings of the critical edition in the 'real world' of manuscripts, where the palaeography and the artwork also contribute to understanding the work in all its forms. It could also be said that the critical edition will itself become a tool for navigating the 'real world' of the manuscripts. In fact all the traditional media of textual scholarship, the bibliography, the collation, the transcription, the edition will have a new role in the age of mass digitization.

The transcription becomes different, since it is no longer the only way by which the user can find out what is written in a manuscript. It will be possible to look at an image of the page. The transcription instead acts first as an explanation to the user of the way in which the editor has reproduced and interpreted that page and secondly as a transferral of selected data from the page into a digital medium. It will be bound to lack some interesting features, and certainly those of interest to a palaeographer or an art historian. When all is said and done, the manuscript page is the most flexible tool for setting out a text. The scribe has control over every element of layout and presentation, since the positioning, shape, size, and colour of every stroke is a scribal decision. By contrast, a printed book has rather a limited range of choices, since although one could produce a virtually unlimited range of character shapes and sizes, in practice if freedom was the goal then it would be easier to make a copy by hand. The digital medium may turn out to have more of the flexibility of the handwritten tradition, once we have worked out how to use it. So far we have hardly got over the threshold.

So, the transcriber has to decide on the relevant data on the manuscript page. Perhaps in the future there will be a way of eliminating the transcription, so that instead the editor will have a range of tools for highlighting and defining elements on the page recorded as an image. Since the Codex Sinaiticus Project we have been able to highlight a word both in an image and in a corresponding transcription. Between the giving of the lectures and this printed version we have developed tools to highlight and tag elements on a page. Perhaps we will have automatic readers clever enough accurately to interpret a complex page with multiple letter forms and abbreviations and corrections and make a digital representation of it. (Such a reader, if it was accurate enough, would reduce the risk of error in the key transition of the material from manuscript page to transcription, which I suggested in the previous lecture was the largest transition in the digital edition.) For the moment it is easier to train someone to do it manually.

The transcription is a symbolic representation, a simplification of the manuscript page. It has two uses. First, it is the bridge between the images and an edition. It is a way for navigating the manuscript and for comparing it with other manuscripts. Secondly, it is a source of information which users can explore in any way they choose. Let us think briefly about the concordance. The traditional printed concordance gave the words that appeared in a printed text.[6] This restricts our horizons to the decisions of editors, and we have no idea how many more (or fewer) times a word might appear in the manuscripts. To have available and searchable the transcriptions of all the manuscripts changes the nature of the concordance, and makes it possible to explore properly the full usage of a word in the entire tradition. Every scholar will be able to get a full picture and determine how restricting the critical edition has been in understanding the usage. The concordance will be a concordance to the work in its historical entirety, not merely in its latest printed manifestation. Such a concordance can also be open to other corpora, so that a word may be studied in an even wider context.

The same applies to orthography: in printed editions, everything is standardized, even in the apparatus. Fully searchable transcriptions make it possible to study spelling customs. In the same way, patterns of correction may be explored, along with density of letters on a page, and anything else that a researcher wants to study.

The furthest we have gone so far with digitizing a manuscript is in our online Codex Sinaiticus.[7]

Codex Sinaiticus

There are four key components to the edition: images, transcription, conservation document, and translations.

Chronologically, the conservation document was the first to be made, because it is essential to prepare a manuscript for digitization by examining it carefully and conserving it. Just how carefully the conservators took this work is illustrated by the documentation. For each page it records data on the following principal topics:

parchment (including thickness, opacity, colour, dimensions)
scribal activity (including pricking marks, ruling)

binding
previous treatment and repairs
condition (including curling, creasing, staining, ink loss)
conservation carried out as a result of survey.

In addition, a mylar sheet was made for each page, onto which were copied the layout of prickings and rulings, and thousands of photographs were taken of details, using a hand-held camera.

For encountering the manuscript, the images take pride of place. Every page was photographed according to the same technical standards, both with light from above and with raking light (with the exception of the fragments, which were too uneven for it to work). One or two heavily fragmented leaves were reconstructed using Photoshop. The images were also used for making a print facsimile edition, published in November 2010.[8]

The transcription provides a detailed interpretation of the images, and the two are linked together so that to click on a word in one is to highlight the same word in the other. This link may be a step towards the remarkable future I have imagined in which the images of a manuscript will be searchable in the same way that a transcription is at present. Following the layout of the manuscript, the transcription also contains pop-up boxes explaining every one of the manuscript's 27,000 corrections.

The translations, currently in their infancy, offer the opportunity for versions of the text, with corrections which can be reproduced in translation, to be in the four languages of the project partners—English, German, Russian, and Greek.

What is this? What kind of edition is it? Lacking reference to any other manuscript, this project set out to explore Codex Sinaiticus fully in its physical and textual complexity and to make it available and intelligible to a new audience.

What did we learn from this project? Technically, we were able to go as far as was possible in recording the detail of a manuscript in a transcription and linking it to images. More generally, we discovered just how popular a Bible manuscript can be. In the first four weeks after its launch in July 2009, the site had over one million unique visitors. By the end of December 2010 this number had grown to over 2 million. I report this fact because it demonstrates that one of the greatest consequences of digitization is the democratization of fields which have hitherto only been accessible to a few people with the resources and opportunity. The country with the fourth highest number of visitors to the Codex Sinaiticus website has been Brazil. The lack of primary resources has hitherto been an obstacle to research there.[9] It seems that the internet has provided Brazilian philologists with some raw material—or even been instrumental in increasing their numbers. This change may have a profound effect on the demography of textual scholarship, making it into a viable pursuit across the globe and no longer the preserve of researchers in countries rich either in manuscripts or in research libraries.

New Testament Transcripts

The online Codex Sinaiticus is an edition of a single manuscript. It shows what one can do in the realm of digitization, description, and transcription. What we did not attempt to do is to compare it with any other documents or texts. That is done elsewhere. As I have said, the transcription is already available in three other online locations, each with different presentation.[10]

One of these, NT Transcripts, gives you a traditional apparatus. But it also gives you the opportunity to see the spelling errors and other 'noise', to compare the witnesses as full lines of text with the differing wordings highlighted in different colours, or to see the transcription of any witness, either in longer lines or according to the manuscript layout. Such a transcription will increasingly be linked to images. This makes it possible for you to break off at any point in the narrative and explore a single part of it in more detail.

NT Transcripts should be every New Testament scholar's first port of call in research. Because it contains transcriptions, it is more use than Nestle-Aland. Anyone who is working on John should use iohannes.com as a matter of course.

The new generation of digital tools also makes possible the baseless collation, to which I referred in the fourth lecture. This has several consequences. One is significant theoretically. In the previous lecture I described the critical text as hooks on which the apparatus is hung. Currently that base text is also the set of hooks inside the database, so that the apparatus only exists once a base text has been determined. Once the baseless apparatus is possible, each form of text and therefore also the variants have their own existence independent of the editorial decisions. There is no requirement to make a base text. All that we need is *word numbers* as an organizing principle. In the printed edition a base text will be there, but as a matter of choice rather than as a necessity.[11] The other consequence is that the user will potentially be able to select any witness as the base text, and to see how the rest of the tradition looks from a new point of view. From that we can imagine future online editions where users will be able to build their own text. We can already present data in multiple formats to suit a particular purpose. Recently, we have been adapting 'open social' freeware for users to build their own layout to work in their own preferred way according to the task in hand. So if we take the three elements of images, transcriptions, and analytical tools, one could envisage any one of them as the organizing element in making an edition, and one could imagine a user selecting the particular element which they wanted to be the focus of their own research. Users will be able to build their own critical text. One could imagine a game of reading selection and text-building as a way of improving one's skills as a philologist.

There is now the opportunity to combine images of manuscripts with detailed descriptions, even to put a link between a comment and that feature in the image. Such features surmount the limitations of the printed book, where such information can only be presented in two dimensions. There is also the facility to mash existing web materials. For example, one could imagine linking information about a scribe known by name from the colophon he wrote and a site such as Prosopography of the Byzantine World.[12] This will be made possible by ensuring that all metadata will be exposed, so that researchers will be able to study it directly, rather than within the limitations of someone else's interface. For example, historians of other aspects of Byzantine culture could use metadata produced in our research in Birmingham and Münster to discover commentaries, transcripts, and images relating to any manuscripts and texts in which they are interested, and to add more information and extend the web of cross-references.

I spoke in the fourth lecture of the importance of keeping transitions to a minimum. This requires a simplified workflow which makes accurate recording and analysis as straightforward as possible. We are beginning to realize this with the Workspace for Collaborative Editing, the online editing tool designed around an integrated workflow, which I described in the fourth lecture. This tool is being developed for one of the most difficult sets of works to edit, due to the number of witnesses and the complicated transmission history.

Anything that works for this material should work for anything else. We hope that the tools we are creating will be taken up and applied to many other sets of manuscripts, be they of the New Testament in another language, of another Greek or Latin text, of a vernacular text, in short of any work in any language.

Where is the traditional critical edition? I have said several times that its role is changing. In the digital environment, it remains important. We have proposed collecting a formidable mass of materials:

an image of every page of every manuscript cited
a full transcription of every manuscript
databases and search and analytical tools for studying it all.

The accusation might be made that in making it possible for the user to test and develop our work we have led them into an apparently pathless wilderness. A map and a compass are needed to reveal that there are paths and that the wilderness is not so wild. The critical edition is both map and compass. Once all the material has been made available, the critical edition and its principles do not become less important but gain a new value because they provide a story and a framework for navigating through the process. Without it I would be adrift in an ocean of data. With it I am equipped to understand the textual history and through it the work which I am studying.

Out of this world will come an even more enriched edition, which will include databases with descriptions of the artistic and palaeographical features and links between connected manuscripts. I said in the third lecture that we have lost most of the environment through which the work has reached us, notably the daily world and conversation of those who made and used the copies. We cannot recreate the entire context of the manuscript tradition, since we have lost the spoken words of any given time, but such a holistic critical edition will do its best to locate the documents and texts in as full an environment as possible.

With images, transcriptions, and the critical edition there are now multiple options before us, each with a different potential focus of interest and therefore the potential to be developed in a different direction. One might say that the images illuminate the document, the transcriptions the text, and the edition the work.

I will illustrate that in a moment, but to avoid getting ahead of myself, let me recap the main steps in making a critical edition which I listed in the fourth lecture. They are:

1. make a list of all known manuscripts
2. acquire microfilm of every manuscript
3. choose the most appropriate manuscripts to be included
4. make full electronic transcriptions of the selected witnesses
5. place the transcriptions in a database and collate them
6. add citations and versional data
7. edit the collation
8. determine the critical text.

How should these tasks be carried out today?

1. Display a database listing all known manuscripts. This should provide facilities for users to alert the database managers to new finds, errors in their information, or additional information about a manuscript. In my view this should include a wiki-style opportunity for users with various levels of accreditation to describe manuscripts, index their contents, and transcribe them. It should also be a much more flexible tool than the existing list. I want to know about the artwork, how many scribes there are, whether there is a colophon and a scribe's name, what paratext there is, whether there are supplementary leaves, whether there are missing

pages. I want to know the contents of every page so that I can go to a particular passage.

2. Include digital images of every manuscript on the website. These can be displayed either through a link to another site or on the edition's server.

3. Display on the website the database and tools with which the manuscripts were selected. The tools should be available so that they may be applied to other manuscript traditions.

4. Transcriptions will from now on be made through a WYSIWYG system, either stored locally or with a live internet link, so that they have to conform to the norms of the edition and are immediately stored securely.[13] This takes care also of the first part of 5.

5. Collation will be undertaken using software which does not require a base text.

6. Citations and versional data are added to the apparatus of Greek witnesses from the citations database.

7. The editor revises the critical apparatus as a result of stages 6 and 7, and determines the critical text using the online editor described in the previous lecture.

The material, such as transcriptions, should be made freely available to users as XML. If it is only made available within an environment created by ourselves, it will only be of value within the tools made for that environment. Instead it must be truly exposed data, which anyone can use however they choose. It seems highly likely that other people will have good ideas about using the material which have not occurred to us.

What the New Testament of the future may be like

The vision I have just outlined for the future takes as its premise the new tools which we either have at our disposal or are building at the moment. These tools are changing the framework of our thought. In the first lecture, one of the things I discussed was the relationship between textual and manuscript studies. In the suite of programmes which I have described, the two come together. The critical edition of the future contains within itself the individual manuscripts, presented as transcriptions and images, *and* the reconstructed Initial Text *and* the analysis of their relationship. This is because, whereas in the past the critical edition contained everything the editor wanted us to know, today the critical edition is a front end to the database in which is what *we* want to know.

As one might say, once the critical edition was the database, now it is the interface.

Such an interface is essential, given the complexity of the data, since the user is entitled to be given the benefit of the editor's detailed experience of it. Raw textual data is like reality—humankind cannot bear very much of it.

CONCLUSIONS

The time has come to draw my thoughts together. How successful have I been at describing the business of making the New Testament? Let me summarize the main themes of each lecture.

In the first I discussed certain general matters concerning the purpose and nature of textual research, setting it in the framework of a hierarchy of documents, texts, and work. I emphasized the importance of including the scribe and the physicality of the manuscript in any study of the New Testament. I also put forward the view that 'Every written work is a process and not an object'. I discussed the concept of a critical text, and suggested that it should not be confused with any supposed 'original' text. I did so first on the grounds that it is an anachronism in respect of earliest Christianity, and secondly with the argument that the concept of an authorial text is a fallacy. Instead, I suggested that the task of the textual scholar is to recover the form of text from which all surviving copies may be shown to be descended. These observations were set within the framework of the view that 'the New Testament' is a concept made possible by editorial theory and practice and not something which self-evidently exists.

In the second lecture I set out to answer the question 'What is a New Testament manuscript?' I discussed papyri, amulets, glossaries, parchment manuscripts, ostraca, lapidary inscriptions, commentaries and catena manuscripts, lectionaries, and paratextual elements. I came to the conclusion that there is no such thing as a New Testament manuscript, and suggested that we should think of documents in terms of the single works or smaller collections which they included. I made the proposal that one could better apply the idea of canonicity to works rather than to documents.

In the third lecture I discussed ways of understanding how manuscripts are related. I did so under the three headings of:

physical evidence for close relationship
comparison of artwork
analysis of the text.

I discussed the traditional problems with stemmatics and described some of the ways in which New Testament scholarship has described the relationships between manuscripts. I paid particular attention to the Coherence-Based Genealogical Method, more easily called the Münster Method, and argued that it solves the traditional problems of stemmatics, notably contamination and coincidence in error. I demonstrated that the Method works by calculating the most likely relationships overall between the manuscripts, called the textual flow.

In the fourth lecture I described the history of the critical edition and discussed the urgent need for today's *Editio critica maior*. I also raised the question of the relationship between an edition and the work. I proposed the view that the work is not identical with the text of a critical edition, the Initial Text, but is found in the sum total of the ways in which it has been transmitted—the entire textual flow. The critical edition is best understood as a narrative, telling the history of the text. I discussed also the way in which it may be used to promulgate the myth of the work existing in a single definitive form in which the multiplicity of its historical forms is suppressed.

In the fifth lecture I discussed the way in which the edition is changing, and with it the way in which all those studying the New Testament find their relationship to the works changing. At present, it is still possible to work with printed materials only, as though the web-based editions did not exist. Whether that will continue to be the case seems very improbable.

Where are we as far as Fredson Bowers' 'General procedures of textual criticism as it deals with manuscript study' are concerned? We saw that in his view they 'have been formulated for some years'. There is undoubtedly a strong continuity in textual scholarship. The Münster Method is based upon traditional stemmatics and philology, and is innovative in making them work better than they have ever done before rather than in replacing them. The *Editio critica maior* and the transcriptions and editorial methods likewise build upon traditional skills. But the general procedures are now different, for two reasons: because of the new tools we have built, and because all our material and all the stages of our work are available for scrutiny and for further use.

One of my conclusions is that the digital environment has led us to discover the significance of the hierarchy of documents, texts, and work. No longer is the printed version of the work all in all, to the extent that the work is identified with the printed edition. Instead, the process of digitization has brought back into full view the documents, and with the documents the individual forms of text found in the documents. Some of the most interesting textual scholarship of the past twenty years has engaged with the variety of these individual forms, treating them not only as sources for reconstructing an oldest recoverable text, but also as a tool for understanding interpretation and use of the New Testament in early Christianity. One thinks of

Bart Ehrman's thesis in *The Orthodox Corruption of Scripture* that scribes sometimes changed the text they copied to bring out the orthodox meaning which must lie behind the apparently heterodox wording.[1] One may consider as even more helpful Jennifer Knust's study of the interplay between textual variation and interpretation in the story of the adulterous woman (John 7.53–8.11).[2] Such research is in its infancy, and it will be exciting to watch it develop.

I here observe that while to some people digital materials are just print materials published in a new medium (this is markedly true of commercial enterprises), to some of us they are new kinds of materials whose creation is actively changing philology.

The appearance of tools which will allow users to make their own texts will weaken the dominance of editorial texts as definitive versions. The question of the impact of multiple privatized versions on the concept of authorized versions to be read in church is, in the 400th anniversary year of the 1611 King James Version, an interesting question. It is certainly true that digital technology has encouraged us to focus on the text as a process and on the edition as a narrative, and is not so interested in a single authoritative text.

It would be regrettable if New Testament scholarship as a whole did not catch on to this, and indeed became instead ever more fixated on a single editorial text, which it mistakenly treats as a first-century authorial text. It is perhaps symptomatic of this that New Testament scholars are rather too wedded to print editions. It seems odd that many of them are not among the 2 million who have visited the Codex Sinaiticus website!

To conclude, let me share with you the things which have excited and surprised me most in preparing and giving these lectures.

First was the discovery of the idea of the text as a process, which I do not think I have formulated before. It came from watching, quite by chance in an idle moment, a programme about waves. Apparently (at least as I remembered it afterwards) almost everything is a wave in some way, and a wave is a process. The reason that the waves of the sea fascinate us is because they are the only ones we can see. This seemed to me a good way of describing the life of a work transmitted in a sequence of textual forms through an untold number of documents.

Second was the opportunity to begin to find out more about the scribe Theodore Hagiopetrites, to whom I hope to return. I would like to find out why his two 1301 copies are so similar in text in Luke and John and not so similar in Matthew and Mark.

More surprising, thirdly, was the realization of my dissatisfaction with Westcott and Hort and the dominance of their theories for so long. The certainty of their conclusions is not justified by the limited extent of their observations. It is curious that today some scholars are so reluctant to abandon the generalizations of the text-type theory, when the complete evidence now available offers a better way.

Fourthly, and, partly apropos Westcott and Hort, I was forcibly struck by the observation that their two 'Neutral' manuscripts, the codices Sinaiticus and Vaticanus differed as many times from each other in James as the thirteenth-century Byzantine manuscript 2423 did from the Initial Text.

Finally, having started with the concept of text as a process, and with the distinction between documents, texts, and work, I believe that I have made some progress towards the goal of understanding the New Testament writings as a set of works containing many forms of text and no single definitive form, which may be described solely by the examination of the manuscripts in which those forms of text are found.

NOTES

Introduction

1. The example is from the *Revised English Bible* (Oxford: Oxford University Press, and Cambridge: Cambridge University Press, 1989), and refers to Acts 13.1–21.26.

2. J. A. H. Murray, *A New English Dictionary on Historical Principles*, vol. 8 (Oxford: Clarendon Press, 1914); under the second definition, 'To write again or anew; to rewrite. Now *rare*', note the reference to T. L. Peacock, 'A careful search will probably discover more than two rescribed leaves.'

Lecture 1

1. F. Bowers, *Bibliography and Literary Criticism: The Lyell Lectures, Oxford, Trinity Term 1959* (Oxford: Clarendon Press, 1964), p. 1.

2. *Textual and Literary Criticism* (Cambridge: Cambridge University Press, 1959), pp. 35–65.

3. P. Maas, *Textual Criticism* (Oxford: Oxford University Press, 1958). This is a translation of *Textkritik*, 3rd edn (Leipzig: Teubner, 1957).

4. Bowers, *Bibliography and Literary Criticism*, pp. 7f.

5. Ibid., pp. 7f. ('only' here disavows any claim thereby to recover an authorial text).

6. It is clear that Erasmus and the other protagonists of the Greek New Testament were so intent on replacing the Latin text with the Greek original, that they did not consider the possibility that a text might be Greek and yet less original than the Latin.

7. The third edition of *The Shorter Oxford English Dictionary* describes the meaning 'One devoted to learning or literature; a scholar' as 'now rare', thus giving priority to its second definition, 'A person versed in the science of language'. C. T. Onions (rev.), *The Shorter Oxford English*

Dictionary on Historical Principles (Oxford: Clarendon Press, 1973); original edition 1944.

8. This non-controversial definition is an important one today, when the virtual worlds of exegesis, textual criticism, and palaeography require that we think carefully about defining the things we make and the ways in which they are related to one another. Its significance is underlined by the fact that 'Documents, works, texts' was the name of a research project funded by JISC and undertaken at ITSEE, in which we defined ontologies for exposing text-related data. The original description was by Peter Robinson.

9. One may consider too the way in which writers make playful use of the possibilities—the long tale in *Alice in Wonderland*, or Sterne's blank page in *Tristram Shandy*.

10. I have explored these questions in more detail in *The Living Text of the Gospels* (Cambridge: Cambridge University Press, 1997).

11. For a brief discussion and further reading, see C. A. Evans, 'Textual Criticism and Textual Confidence: How Reliable is Scripture?', in R. B. Stewart (ed.), *The Reliability of the New Testament: Bart D. Ehrman and Daniel B. Wallace in Dialogue* (Minneapolis: Fortress, 2011), pp. 161–72, 164f.

12. See, for example, *Contra Faustum* 32.16, where Augustine refers to errors in Latin codices being corrected against older ones or Greek copies. See H. A. G. Houghton, *Augustine's Text of John: Patristic Citations and Latin Gospel Manuscripts* (Oxford: Oxford University Press, 2008), p. 19.

13. There is a reference in Galen's Περὶ Ἀλυπησίας (a writing rediscovered in 2005) to αὐτόγραφα (autographs). According to the editors, this is possibly a textual corruption for ἀντίγραφα (copies) (V. Boudon-Millot and J. Jouanna with A. Pietrobelli (eds), *Galen, Œeuvres,* vol. 4: *Ne pas se chagriner* (Paris: Editions Belles Lettres, 2010). But the passage in question (Περὶ Ἀλυπησίας 13ff.), which explains that the fire of 192 destroyed not only Galen's own books but the books in the Palatine libraries which he had used, does certainly show Galen seeking 'good copies' by searching out critical editions by named

editors which were renowned for the quality of their text (13), and also editing his own texts (14). My thanks to my colleague Dr Rosalind MacLachlan for this information.

14. The compilation of larger collections of the Gospels or letters will include a certain degree of standardization, for example of title, and certainly of layout. Thus the original independence of the writing is to some extent subsumed into the necessary homogeneity of a larger collection. In the case of the letters attributed to Paul, it even involved attributing the genre of letter to a writing which is not a letter and not by Paul, namely the so-called Epistle to the Hebrews. In the case of Philemon, its original single-sheet status was lost.

15. M. Dibelius, *Die Formgeschichte des Evangeliums* (Tübingen: Mohr (Siebeck), 1919) [ET: *From Tradition to Gospel* (London: Ivor Nicholson and Watson, 1934)]; K. L. Schmidt, *Der Rahmen der Geschichte Jesu: Literarkritische Untersuchungen zur ältesten Jesusüberlieferung* (Berlin: Trowitzsch, 1919); R. Bultmann, *Die Geschichte der synoptischen Tradition* (Göttingen: Vandenhoek & Ruprecht, 1921) [ET: *The History of the Synoptic Tradition* (Oxford: Blackwell, 1963)].

16. G. Bornkamm, G. Barth, and H. J. Held, *Überlieferung und Auslegung im Matthäusevangelium* (Neukirchen: Kreis Moers, 1960) [ET: *Tradition and Interpretation in Matthew* (London: SCM Press, 1963)]; H. Conzelmann, *Die Mitte der Zeit: Studien zur Theologie des Lukas* (Tübingen: Mohr, 1954) [ET: *The Theology of St Luke* (London: Faber & Faber, 1960)].

17. Members of von Soden's K^r group (see H. von Soden, *Die Schriften des Neuen Testaments in ihrer ältesten erreichbaren Textgestalt hergestellt auf Grund ihrer Textgeschichte*, vol. 2 (Berlin: Arthur Glaue, 1907), pp. 757–65 are similar in orthography to modern standards. Most noteworthy are the Paris manuscripts, Bibliothèque Nationale Gr. 47 (Gregory-Aland 18) and especially Coislin Gr. 199 (Gregory-Aland 35).

18. The terms 'lower' and 'higher criticism' came into use in English in the nineteenth century. The former is sometimes mistakenly treated as though its scope was only textual criticism. For just one of the myriad examples showing this to be wrong, see E. C. Colwell, 'Biblical Criticism: Lower and Higher', *Journal of Biblical Literature* 67 (1948), pp. 1–12.

19. The origins of palaeography lie in the beginnings of the scientific edition in the earliest phase of the Enlightenment, particularly in the work of the Maurists.

20. See, for example, *The Living Text of the Gospels*.

21. D. C. Parker and S. R. Pickering (eds), Oxyrhynchus Papyrus 4968, in D. Leith, D. C. Parker, S. R. Pickering, et al. (eds), *The Oxyrhynchus Papyri*, vol. 74 (London: Egypt Exploration Society, 2009), pp. 1–45. For the endings of Romans, see H. Y. Gamble, *The Textual History of the Letter to the Romans*, Studies and Documents 42 (Grand Rapids: Eerdmans, 1977).

22. R. Bentley, letter to Archbishop Wake, 1716, in A. Dyce (ed.), *Richard Bentley: The Works*, vol. 3 (London, 1838; repr. Hildesheim and New York: Olms, 1971), pp. 477–9, 477. The letter was first printed in 1807.

23. *Novum Testamentum Graecum: Editio critica maior*, ed. Institut für Neutestamentliche Textforschung, IV: *Die Katholischen Briefe*, ed. B. Aland, K. Aland†, G. Mink, H. Strutwolf, and K. Wachtel (Stuttgart: Deutsche Bibelgesellschaft, 1997–2005). See my chapter 'Is "Living Text" Compatible with "Initial Text"? Editing the Gospel of John', in K. Wachtel and M. W. Holmes (eds), *The Textual History of the Greek New Testament: Changing Views in Contemporary Research*, Society of Biblical Literature, Text-Critical Studies 8 (Atlanta: Society of Biblical Literature, 2011), pp. 13–21.

24. http://www.jisc.ac.uk/whatwedo/programmes/inf11/jiscexpo.aspx (accessed 3 March 2011).

25. I must add an apology to the reader that I am unable to be so generous within the confines of a printed book.

26. Katherine Swift, *The Morville Hours* (London: Bloomsbury, 2008), p. 289.

27. This first lecture was followed by a reception and dinner.

Lecture 2

1. See http://intf.uni-muenster.de/vmr/NTVMR/ListeHandschriften. php (accessed 10 March 2011). This is the number of manuscripts, and takes into account the allocation of several numbers to different parts of the same artefact. Even so, these numbers will never be precise. For

example, Metropolitan Museum of Art, Department of Egyptian Art 14.1.527 (Gregory-Aland P⁴⁴) is really two manuscripts, which would bring the number of papyri up to 126. Some minuscules are two manuscripts bound together (for example, one might find an Apocalypse with a copy of Acts and the epistles). See D. C. Parker, *An Introduction to the New Testament Manuscripts and their Texts* (Cambridge: Cambridge University Press, 2008), pp. 77–8.

2. The youngest dated manuscript (according to K. Aland with M. Welte, B. Köster, and K. Junack, *Kurzgefasste Liste der griechischen Handschriften des Neuen Testaments*, Arbeiten zur Neutestamentlichen Textforschung 1, 2nd edn (Berlin and New York: De Gruyter, 1994)) is Gregory-Aland 2887 (Athos, Panteleimonos 661), which was written in 1888. It is said to be a copy of Gregory-Aland 1160 (Patmos, Ioannou 58), of the twelfth century. If so, it has no independent value. It is not the only nineteenth-century manuscript in the catalogue, and one other is also dated, to the year 1830 (Gregory-Aland 2267, St Petersburg, Russian Academy, Collection of the Russian Institute of Constantinople 165).

3. There are fewer than a dozen examples dated between the fourth and seventh centuries.

4. C. R. Gregory, *Textkritik des Neuen Testamentes*, 3 vols (Leipzig: J. C. Hinrichs, 1900–9); C. Tischendorf, *Novum Testamentum Graece . . . Editio octava critica maior*, vol. 3: *Prolegomena*, by C. R. Gregory (Leipzig: J. C. Hinrichs, 1884).

5. Oxford, Ashmolean Museum Papyrus Oxyrhynchus 2684. It may be viewed online at http://intf.uni-muenster.de/vmr/NTVMR/viewer/viewerCodex01.php. See T. Wasserman, 'P⁷⁸ (P. Oxy. XXXIV 2684)—The Epistle of Jude on an Amulet?', in T. J. Kraus and T. Nicklas (eds), *New Testament Manuscripts: Their Texts and their World*, Texts and Editions for New Testament Study 2 (Leiden: E. J. Brill, 2006), pp. 137–60.

6. Vienna, Österreichische Nationalbibliothek, P. 2312.

7. See Parker, *An Introduction to the New Testament Manuscripts*, pp. 42, 126.

8. See S. R. Pickering, 'The Significance of Non-Continuous New Testament Textual Materials in Papyri', in D. G. K. Taylor (ed.), *Studies in the Early Text of the Gospels and Acts*, Texts and Studies Third

Series 1 (Birmingham: Birmingham University Press, 1999), pp. 121–41; S. E. Porter, 'Textual Criticism in the Light of Diverse Textual Evidence for the Greek New Testament: An Expanded Proposal', in T. J. Kraus and T. Nicklas (eds), *New Testament Manuscripts: Their Texts and their World*, Texts and Editions for New Testament Study 2 (Leiden: E. J. Brill, 2006), pp. 305–37.

9. T. Wasserman, 'Papyrus 72 and the *Bodmer Miscellaneous Codex*', *New Testament Studies* 51 (2005), pp. 137–54. Revised as *The Epistle of Jude: Its Text and Transmission*, Coniectanea Biblica, New Testament Series 43 (Lund: Almqvist & Wiksell International, 2006), pp. 30–50.

10. T. Nicklas and T. Wasserman, 'Theologische Linien im *Codex Bodmer Miscellani*? [*sic*]', in J. Kraus and Nicklas (eds), *New Testament Manuscripts: Their Texts and their World*, Texts and Editions for New Testament studies 2 (Leiden: E. J. Brill, 2006), pp. 161–88.

11. See D. C. Parker, *Codex Bezae, An Early Christian Manuscript and its Text* (Cambridge: Cambridge University Press, 1992), pp. 51–9, with further bibliography, now to be supplemented from J. K. Elliott, *A Bibliography of Greek New Testament Manuscripts*, Society for New Testament Studies, Monograph Series 62, 2nd edn (Cambridge: Cambridge University Press, 2000), p. 39. For the further history of glossaries in New Testament manuscripts, see D. Jongkind, 'Some Observations on the Relevance of the "Early Byzantine Glossary" of Paul for the Textual Criticism of the *Corpus Paulinum*', *Novum Testamentum* 53 (2011), pp. 358–75.

12. Codex Sinaiticus: London, British Library, Add. Ms. 43725 + Leipzig, Universitätsbibliothek Gr. 1 + St Petersburg, National Library of Russia Gr. 2, 259 + Sinai, Monastery of St Catherine, New Find MΓ 1 (Gregory-Aland 01); Codex Alexandrinus: (London, British Library, Royal Ms. 1 D.V–VIII (Gregory-Aland 02). See further D. C. Parker, *Codex Sinaiticus: The Story of the World's Oldest Bible* (London: British Library, and Peabody, MA: Hendrikson, 2010), pp. 29–39; S. McKendrick, *In a Monastery Library: Preserving Codex Sinaiticus and the Greek Written Heritage* (London: British Library, 2006).

13. Codex Bezae also contains *hermeneiai*, as does the Latin Codex Sangermanensis (for bibliography, see Parker, *Codex Bezae*, p. 43). But in both these manuscripts they were added much later. What is distinctive

about the manuscripts I have in mind is that the *hermeneiai* are integral to the original composition.

14. Yale University, Beinecke Library Dura Pg. 24 (formerly P. Dura 24) (Gregory-Aland 0212).

15. E. Nestle, *Einführung in das griechische Neue Testament*, 4th edn, rev. E. von Dobschütz, (Göttingen: Vandenhoeck & Ruprecht, 1923), p. 86. Further bibliography in Elliott, *A Bibliography of Greek New Testament Manuscripts*, p. 80.

16. So I said in the lecture. Since then, Christian Askeland has clearly demonstrated that the very incomplete text can only be made into the Pericope Adulterae by some very implausible reconstruction. It is more likely to refer to litigation surrounding a marriage. The history of research of the fragment is fascinating and so I retain the reference, even though my original purpose in discussing the ostracon is exploded.

17. C. E. Römer, 'Ostraka mit christlichen Texten aus der Sammlung Flinders Petrie', *Zeitschrift für Papyrologie und Epigraphik* 145 (2003), pp. 183–201, 186.

18. G. Lefebvre, 'Fragments grecs des Evangiles', *Bulletin de l'Institut français d'archéologie orientale* 4 (1905), pp. 1–15. See http://www.trismegistos. org/ldab/text.php?tm=61837. Note that the ostracon joins the mere sixteen Greek manuscripts which omit Luke 22.43–4.

19. My thanks to Dr Walter Cockle for this information.

20. The word is εὐσηβήστατος; Codex Sinaiticus and a few other manuscripts read εὐσεβής. For further details, see E. Puech, 'Le tombeau de Siméon et Zacharie dans la vallée de Josaphat', *Revue Biblique* 111 (2004), pp. 563–77, and Parker, *An Introduction to the New Testament Manuscripts*, pp. 128f.

21. I have noted elsewhere the occasional appearance in the *Liste* of a manuscript in modern Greek. See Parker, *An Introduction to the New Testament Manuscripts*, p. 41.

22. Such customs may have been modified by the subsequent copying tradition of the commentary, leading to either more or less text being present in many or even all the manuscripts (in the latter case we might be hard-pressed to know the commentator's practice). We have also to be alert to the possibility that the editors of modern editions

may have standardized the biblical lemmata to their own sense of what is proper, or even added lemmata where there were none in the manuscript tradition. A member of the audience noted that a critical edition of Gildas' *De excidio Britanniae* altered his biblical citations from the wordings in the manuscripts to those in a printed Vulgate.

23. Cambridge University Library, British and Foreign Bible Society Ms 213 (Gregory-Aland 040).

24. Vatican, Ottob. gr. 432 (Gregory-Aland 391).

25. Munich, Universitätsbibliothek 2° Cod. ms. 30 (Gregory-Aland 033). Other manuscripts with a similar presentation have been placed under the minuscule category.

26. Such as Vatican gr. 1618 (Gregory-Aland 377).

27. E.g. Vatican Barb. gr. 521 (Gregory-Aland 392).

28. Alfred Tennyson, 'Merlin and Vivien', *Idylls of the King*.

29. J. Reuss, *Matthäus-, Markus- u. Johannes-Katenen nach den handschriftlichen Quellen untersucht*, Neutestamentliche Abhandlungen 18/4–5 (Münster: Aschendorf, 1941). I will venture to say that I suspect Reuss' classification. I have no evidence for this, except that it seems very formalized and I suspect that the catena tradition may have been looser than that. It is true that his conclusions have never been subjected to scrutiny and have thus never been verified.

30. We should not forget that catena manuscripts may also be significant witnesses to patristic texts. Sometimes they contain citations from lost works, and their citations of known works do not necessarily conform to the texts of the printed editions.

31. They are Vatican, Barb. gr. 495 (Gregory-Aland 849) and 504 (Gregory-Aland 850), Vatican gr. 592 (Gregory-Aland 1819) and 593 (Gregory-Aland 1820), and Venice, Biblioteca Nazionale Marciana Gr. Z. 121 (324) (Gregory-Aland 2129).

32. These are the places listed in his index: Berlin, Bologna, Budapest (one unexamined manuscript), Florence, Jerusalem, Milan (two libraries), Moscow, Munich (two libraries), Oxford, Paris, Rome (three libraries), Toledo, Turin, the Vatican, Venice, Vienna.

33. See Reuss, *Matthäus-, Markus- U. Johannes-Katenen*, pp. 196–204.

34. K. Aland†, B. Aland, and K. Wachtel, with K. Witte (eds), *Text und Textwert der griechischen Handschriften des Neuen Testaments*, V: *Das Johannesevangelium*, Arbeiten zur Neutestamentlichen Forschung 35–6 (Berlin and New York: De Gruyter, 2005), pp. 32–3.

35. Ibid., p. 33. But note that it scores a little less highly if one counts only those readings where Nestle-Aland and the Majority Text differ. The printed edition is B. Aland, K. Aland, J. Karavidopoulos, C. M. Martini, and B. M. Metzger (eds), *Novum Testamentum Graece*, 27th edn, 8th (rev.) impression (Stuttgart: Deutsche Bibelgesellschaft, 2001).

36. K. Aland†, et al. (eds), *Text und Textwert*, p. 41.

37. Available at http://intf.uni-muenster.de/TT_PP/TT_Clusters.html.

38. This is using the setting 'strict grouping', which eliminates those manuscripts which have a higher level of agreement with the Majority Text.

39. Reuss dates it to the sixteenth or seventeenth century.

40. See Figure 3.5.

41. 850 (see note 31) is excluded from the test passages on the grounds that it does not have continuous text. There looks to be a further anomaly here.

42. Space precludes a further consideration of the other two manuscripts for which there is evidence, 1819 and 2129. Suffice it to say that neither has as striking a text as 849, and that the two are more closely related to each other than to any other manuscript.

43. This observation broadens the range of genres within the Gregory-Aland papyrus category. From information presented by Jennifer Knust and Tommy Wasserman at the Society of Biblical Literature Annual Meeting in San Francisco, 2011.

44. J. Cozza, *Sacrorum Bibliorum uetustissima fragmenta graeca et latina ex palimpsestis codicibus Bibliothecae Cryptoferratensis eruta, Pars 2* (Rome: Spithoever, 1867), p. 336. The lection is first in Greek then in Latin, and was read on Easter Day. The Latin version follows a Vulgate text to verse 14, after which it becomes an *ad hoc* rendering of the Greek.

45. C. R. D. Jordan, 'The Textual Tradition of the Gospel of John in Greek Gospel Lectionaries from the Middle Byzantine Period (8th–11th century)' (Birmingham University, unpublished PhD thesis, 2010).

46. For example, continuous-text manuscripts sometimes contain a lec-
    tionary apparatus, though using such a manuscript in this way is quite
    a complicated procedure. Lectionary manuscripts sometimes contain
    the marginal numbers of the Eusebian Apparatus, although this is use-
    less in such a context. And, to add a further twist, Michael Clark has
    pointed out to me that the catena manuscript Munich, Bayerische
    Staatsbibliothek Gr. 465 (Gregory-Aland 427) has occasional lection-
    ary information.

47. The Gregory-Aland number is L351. See further J. Lowden, *The Jaha-
    ris Gospel Lectionary: The Story of a Byzantine Book* (New York: The
    Metropolitan Museum of Art, and New Haven and London: Yale
    University Press, 2009).

48. L. C. Willard, *A Critical Study of the Euthalian Apparatus*, Arbeiten zur
    neutestamentlichen Textforschung 41 (Berlin and New York: De
    Gruyter, 2009). The only edition ever to have been made was pub-
    lished in 1698: L. A. Zacagni, *Collectanea Monumentorum Veterum
    Ecclesiae ... 4 Euthalii Episc. Sulcensis Actuum Apostolorum, & quatuor-
    decim S. Pauli, aliarumque septem Catholicarum epistolarum edi-
    tio ...* (Rome: Sacrae Congregationis de Propaganda Fide, 1698), pp.
    401–708. Most recently, see V. Blomkvist, 'The Euthalian Apparatus:
    Text, Translation, Commentary' (University of Oslo, doctoral dis-
    sertation, 2011).

49. They are: Poitiers, Bibliothèque Municipale 17 (65) (Old Latin manu-
    script 39), Vendôme, Bibliothèque Municipale 2 (Old Latin manu-
    script 40), and Laon, Bibliothèque Municipale 437 bis (Old Latin
    manuscript 46).

50. P. H. Burton, H. A. G. Houghton, R. F. MacLachlan, and D. C. Parker
    (eds), *Vetus Latina: Die Reste der altlateinischen Bibel nach Petrus Sabatier
    neu gesammelt und herausgegeben von der Erzabtei Beuron unter der Leitung
    von Roger Gryson*, 19: *Johannes* (Freiburg: Herder, 2011–).

51. Already in three centuries we have had a system of numbering which
    used upper-case letters for majuscules, and separate sets of letters and
    numbers for each of the major divisions of the New Testament. We
    have also had a system, recently abandoned, of indicating manuscripts

which are (believed to be) known copies of another being given the same number with the superscript addition of 'abs' (for Abschrift).

52. The links are http://intf.uni-muenster.de/vmr/NTVMR/Index NTVMR.php and http://www.vmr.bham.ac.uk/.

53. There are fewer than fifty out of 3,300 continuous-text manuscripts which were written at one time and contain the whole New Testament and nothing else.

54. I have put the library number as well as the Gregory-Aland number in referring to manuscripts of New Testament works in order to avoid treating them as a separate class.

55. As a result of the parchment codex.

Lecture 3

1. 2nd edn (London: Routledge, 2006), p. 3.

2. See Parker, *An Introduction to the New Testament Manuscripts*, pp. 286–301.

3. R. I. Pervo, *Profit with Delight: The Literary Genre of the Acts of the Apostles* (Philadelphia: Fortress Press, 1987).

4. I suppose that one might have to add the qualification that occasionally one finds a miniature long divorced from its parent manuscript.

5. For example, the group of Byzantine manuscripts of the Gospels known as Family 13.

6. R. S. Nelson, *Theodore Hagiopetrites: A Late Byzantine Scribe and Illuminator*, 2 vols, Veröffentlichungen der Kommission für Byzantinistik 4 (Vienna: Österreichische Akademie der Wissenschaften, 1991). See also von Soden (vol. 2, pp. 781–93).

7. Both von Soden (vol. 1, p. 264, entry $\Theta^{\epsilon 300}$) and the *Liste* give a date: the former has 1280, the latter 1279/80. Vogel and Gardthausen have it as undated: M. Vogel and V. Gardthausen, *Die griechischen Schreiber des Mittelalters und der Renaissance* (Leipzig: Harrassowitz, 1909; repr. Hildesheim: Georg Olms, 1966).

8. With regard to the Gospels manuscript Athos, Iviron 654 (30) (Gregory-Aland 998), von Soden (vol. 1, p. 187, entry ε1385) notes 'Die Unterschrift fol. 210: ο γραφευς ταπεινος Θεοδωρος ο Αγιοπετριτης ist Fälschung einer späterer Hand.' Nelson suggests it may be from Theodore's workshop

(pp. 95f.). For some reason, the scribe left folios 169r to 177v blank, so that the text breaks off at Luke 23.3 ἀποκριθεὶς and resumes at John 7.14 καὶ ἐδίδασκεν. The blank pages are probably sufficient to contain only half the missing text.

9. K. Aland†, et al. (eds), *Text und Textwert*. For the evidence from other Gospels cited below, see, in the same series, IV: *Die Synoptischen Evangelien*, 1: *Das Markusevangelium*, Arbeiten zur Neutestamentlichen Text forschung 26–7 (1998); 2: *Das Matthäusevangelium*, Arbeiten zur Neutestamentlichen Text Forschung 28–9 (1999); 3: *Das Lukasevangelium*, Arbeiten zur Neutestamentlichen Textforschung 30–1 (1999).

10. Athos, Dochiariu 49 (Gregory-Aland 972), of the eleventh century and Athos, Kutlumusiu 73 (Gregory-Aland 1052) of the thirteenth.

11. There are nine differences between them out of 196 test passages in Mark, and in Matthew eight out of 64.

12. C. Tischendorf, *Bibliorum Codex Sinaiticus Petropolitanus*, 1: *Prolegomena* (Leipzig : Giesecke & Devrient, 1862), p. 8.

13. It is not easy to study the scribes of the Vaticanus because the letters have been re-inked.

14. T. C. Skeat, 'The Codex Sinaiticus, the Codex Vaticanus and Constantine', *Journal of Theological Studies* 50 (1999), pp. 583–625; reprinted in J. K. Elliott (ed.), *The Collected Biblical Writings of T. C. Skeat*, Supplement to Novum Testamentum 113 (Leiden and Boston: E. J. Brill, 2004), pp. 193–237, p. 214.

15. I am indebted to my colleague Dr Rachel Kevern for these observations.

16. Annemarie Weyl Carr, *Byzantine Illumination, 1150–1250: The Study of a Provincial Tradition* (Chicago: University of Chicago Press, 1987).

17. This was argued with regard to early Christianity by B. H. Streeter, *The Four Gospels: A Study of Origins Treating of the Manuscript Tradition, Sources, Authorship, & Dates* (London: Macmillan, 1924).

18. K. Maxwell, 'The Afterlife of Texts: Decorative Style Manuscripts and New Testament Textual Criticism', in L. Jones (ed.), *Images and Afterlife: Essays in Honor of Annemarie Weyl Carr* (Aldershot: Ashgate Press, forthcoming).

19. *Novum Testamentum Graecum: Editio critica maior*, ed. Institut für Neutesta-mentliche Textforschung (Stuttgart: Deutsche Bibelgesellschaft, 1997–).

20. F. H. A. Scrivener, *A Plain Introduction to the Criticism of the New Testa-ment for the Use of Biblical Students*, 2 vols, 4th edn, rev. E. Miller (Lon-don and New York: George Bell, and Cambridge: Deighton Bell, 1894), vol. 2, p. 211.

21. Ibid., pp. 224–6.

22. S. Timpanaro, *The Genesis of Lachmann's Method*, ed. and tr. G. W. Most (Chicago and London: University of Chicago Press, 2005), p. 140. This is a translation of *La genesi del metodo del Lachmann*, 2nd edn (Turin: Liviana Editrice, 1981). Original edition 1963.

23. Ibid., p. 65.

24. Ibid., p. 18, citing Bengel.

25. Ibid., p. 66.

26. For example, B. M. Metzger and B. D. Ehrman, *The Text of the New Testament: Its Transmission, Corruption, and Restoration*, 4th edn (Oxford: Oxford University Press, 2005), p. 306.

27. An indicative error is one which cannot have arisen twice by chance, whose presence in several witnesses indicates a direct line of descent between them.

28. B. F. Westcott and F. J. A. Hort, *The New Testament in the Original Greek*, 2 vols (London: Macmillan, 1881), vol. 2, introduction.

29. I have drawn attention elsewhere to the problems with the theory so far as the inconsistency of the groups goes (Parker, *An Introduction to the New Testament Manuscritpts*, pp. 171–4). There are so few manuscripts from the first seven centuries, so few survivors from the thousands that must once have existed, that they cannot be classified into groups. The opposite problem prevails with the Byzantine text, where we have for some works 1,500 documents. Here the differences between them are often so slight that the distance between closely and distantly related copies may come down to a few variations.

30. Streeter, *The Four Gospels*.

31. It is quite strange that New Testament philology drew up a concept of text types based upon the Gospels, and then assumed that it applied to

the entire corpus of writings, even though it has always been widely acknowledged that the text types of the Gospels could not be shown to exist in other parts of the New Testament. Thus we have worked with a very incomplete and unproven system, and in effect tried to reconstruct the oldest recoverable form of the writings without having a sound methodology for doing so.

32. It is also somewhat alarming that in presenting the evidence they begin by 'premising that we do not attempt to notice every petty variant in the passages cited, for fear of confusing the substantive evidence' (p. 95). We therefore do not know how they have distorted the evidence by simplifying it.

33. Westcott and Hort, *The New Testament in the Original Greek*, pp. 145f.

34. At http://intf.uni-muenster.de/cbgm/en.html. For a description of the method by its creator, see G. Mink, 'Contamination, Coherence, and Coincidence in Textual Transmission', in K. Wachtel and M. W. Holmes (eds), *The Textual History of the Greek New Testament: Changing Views in Contemporary Research*, Society of Biblical Literature, Text-Critical Studies 8 (Atlanta: Society of Biblical Literature, 2011), pp. 141–216.

35. Every word has an even number and every space an odd number.

36. Under the influence of the phrase elsewhere in the epistle at 1.16, 19; 2.5.

37. The analogy is found already in G. Zuntz, *The Text of the Epistles: A Disquisition upon the Corpus Paulinum*, The Schweich Lectures 1946 (London: The British Academy, 1953), p. 214, and in the fold-out chart at the back entitled 'An attempt at a graphic presentation of the "stream of the tradition".'

38. It goes without saying that accidentals such as orthographica and nonsense readings are not treated as variant readings.

39. Durham, NC, Duke University Library Gr. 3 (Gregory-Aland 2423), thirteenth century. It is on the right-hand side of Figure 3.5, half way down.

40. Of course, as I observed earlier, the date of a *document* is not necessarily the date of its *text*.

41. Eleventh century, Vienna, Österreichische Nationalbibliothek Theol. gr. 302, fol. 1–353.

42. If there had been no contamination, then all the textual flow would be in a single direction, with the exception of those places where a reading had arisen on two or more separate occasions.

43. It is worth remembering that the more manuscripts are included in an apparatus, the more variants there will be attested only by one or a few manuscripts, and so the percentage difference between the manuscripts will decrease. See the information about John 18, pages 15–16 above.

44. By 'us' I refer to me and Klaus Wachtel of the Münster Institute.

45. Perhaps the best-known example of this is the Codex Sinaiticus, which, it has been argued, is descended from one ancestor in the first seven chapters of John and another in the rest of the Gospel. See G. D. Fee, 'Codex Sinaiticus in the Gospel of John: A Contribution to Methodology in Establishing Textual Relationships', *New Testament Studies* 15 (1968), pp. 23–44.

46. My thanks to Klaus Wachtel for a discussion in which I put this question to him.

Lecture 4

1. D. C. Parker, U. B. Schmid, and W. J. Elliott (eds), *The New Testament in Greek IV: The Gospel According to St. John, Edited by the American and British Committees of the International Greek New Testament Project*, vol. 2: *The Majuscules*, New Testament Tools, Studies and Documents 37 (Leiden: E. J. Brill, 2007). Web edition at http://itsee.bham.ac.uk/iohannes/majuscule/index.html.

2. M. W. Holmes (ed.), *The Greek New Testament: SBL Edition* (Atlanta: Society of Biblical Literature, and Bellingham, WA: Logos Bible Software, 2010).

3. It does occasionally mark alternative readings, but it does not give the manuscript support for any variant.

4. C. Tischendorf, *Novum Testamentum Graece ... Editio octava critica maior*, vols 1–2 (Leipzig: J. C. Hinrichs, 1869–72).

5. K. Lachmann, *Novum Testamentum Graece* (Berlin: Reimer, 1831); *Novum Testamentum Graece et Latine*, 2 vols (Berlin: Reimer, 1842–50); S. P. Tregelles, *The Greek New Testament* (London: Bagster/Stewart,

1857–79); B. F. Westcott and F. J. A. Hort, *The New Testament in the Original Greek* 2 vols (London: Macamillan, 1881).

6. J. Mill, *Η Καινή Διαθήκη* etc. (Oxford, 1707); C. F. Matthaei, *Novum Testamentum Graece et Latine* (Riga, 1782–88). One might add (in respect only of his Prolegomena) von Soden.

7. It may be that the title of B. M. Metzger's influential *The Text of the New Testament: Its Transmission, Corruption, and Restoration* (New York: Oxford University Press, 1964) (which ran to three further editions in 1968, 1972, and 1992) encapsulates this assumption.

8. F. G. Kenyon, *The Chester Beatty Biblical Papyri: Descriptions and Texts of the Twelve Manuscripts on Papyrus of the Greek Bible* (London: Emery Walker, 1934–7). It includes 1: General Introduction; 2: The Gospels and Acts; 3: Pauline Epistles and Revelation; Supplement: Pauline Epistles. There are subsequent volumes of other papyri.

9. V. Martin, *Papyrus Bodmer II: Evangile de Jean chap. 1–14* (Cologny-Geneva: Bibliotheca Bodmeriana, 1956); *Papyrus Bodmer II: Supplément. Evangile de Jean chap. 14–21* (1958), rev. edn with J. W. B. Barns (1962); V. Martin and R. Kasser, *Papyrus Bodmer XIV: Evangile de Luc chap. 3–24; Papyrus Bodmer XV: Evangile de Jean chap. 1–15* (Cologny-Geneva: Bibliotheca Bodmeriana, 1961).

10. B. P. Grenfell and A. S. Hunt, *The Oxyrhynchus Papyri* (London: Egypt Exploration Fund, 1898–). For the papyrus of the Apocalypse see W. E. H. Cockle (ed.), vol. 66 (1999), pp. 10–37. For the Acts papyrus see D. C. Parker and S. R. Pickering (eds), vol. 74 (2009), pp. 1–45; G. Gäbel, 'The Text of 𝔓127 (P. Oxy. 4968) and its Relationship with the Text of Codex Bezae', *Novum Testamentum* 53 (2011), pp. 107–52.

11. A. Merk (ed.), *Novum Testamentum Graece et Latine* (Rome: Pontifical Biblical Institute, 1933) and further editions; J. M. Bover, *Novi Testamenti: Biblia Graeca et Latina* (Madrid: Consejo Superior de Investigaciones Científicas, 1943) and further editions.

12. Aland K., M. Black, B. M. Metzger, and A. Wikgren, *The Greek New Testament* (New York: United Bible Societies, 1966).

13. The problems in the selection of commentary manuscripts to which I referred in the second lecture are an exception.

14. Except Revelation. This will be undertaken by the team at Wuppertal. For further details of the series see Lecture 3, note 9.

15. The tools are continually being developed, and so any detailed information given here would soon be out of date.

16. This has been applied in the selection of manuscripts for the edition of John.

17. See http://www.tei-c.org/index.xml.

18. In the online Codex Sinaiticus at http://www.codexsinaiticus.org/ en/manuscript.aspx; in the online editions of John's Gospel at http:// www.iohannes.com/; in IGNTP Transcripts at http://www.iohannes. com/XML/; and in the Münster part of the Virtual Manuscript Room at http://nttranscripts.uni-muenster.de/.

19. See http://www.vmr.birmingham.ac.uk/itsee/2011/07/09/workspace-update/. The partners are ITSEE (University of Birmingham), the Institut für neutestamentliche Textforschung (University of Münster), and the Kompetenzzentrum für elektronische Erschließungs- und Publikationsverfahren in den Geisteswissenschaften (University of Trier).

20. See Lecture 2, note 22.

21. S. C. E. Legg, *Nouum Testamentum Graece secundum textum Westcotto-Hortianum, Euangelium secundum Marcum* (Oxford: Oxford University Press, 1935); *Euangelium secundum Matthaeum* (1940).

22. *The New Testament in Greek III: The Gospel According to St. Luke, Edited by the American and British Committees of the International Greek New Testament Project*, 2 vols (Oxford: Oxford University Press, 1984–7).

23. I will not attempt to explain the technical basis for this advance, which is the brainchild of staff at the Huygens Institute working on the CollateX Project.

24. Readers interested in volunteering to transcribe manuscripts or to do other work can contact the project at http://www.igntp.org/.

Lecture 5

1. *Η Καινη Διαθηκη. Novum Testamentum ex regiis aliisque optimis editionibus cum cura expressa* (Leiden: Elzevir, 1633): 'textum ergo habes nunc ab omnibus receptum, in quo nihil immutatum aut corruptum damus'.

2. See http://www.bl.uk/manuscripts/.

3. For example, www.e-codices.unifr.ch/en.

4. See http://www.vmr.bham.ac.uk/. Note that users are advised to install Firefox (freely available) in order to access the website most easily.

5. See http://www.csntm.org/.

6. And occasionally in a couple of printed texts (see e.g. W. F. Moulton and A. S. Geden, *A Concordance to the Greek Testament* (Edinburgh, T. & T. Clark, 1897), which has often been reprinted and revised).

7. See http://www.codexsinaiticus.org/en/.

8. *Codex Sinaiticus: A Facsimile* (London: British Library, and Peabody, MA: Hendrickson, 2010).

9. There is only one Greek New Testament manuscript in the country: Rio de Janeiro, Biblioteca Nacionale I.2, (Gregory-Aland 2437).

10. They are: IGNTP Transcripts (http://arts-itsee.bham.ac.uk/itseeweb/iohannes/IGNTPtranscripts/), the edition of the Gospel of John (http://www.iohannes.com/), and in Münster (http://nttranscripts.uni-muenster.de/). These are the links in late 2011. By the time this is published, they may instead all be available together in the Virtual Manuscript Room.

11. Given the absence of word division throughout most of the Greek manuscript tradition, the division into words is itself arguably a modern intervention, so that the imposition of numbers based upon words cannot be for any reason other than our convenience. It is not integral to the work.

12. See http://www.pbw.kcl.ac.uk/.

13. Developed for the Workspace in 2011.

Conclusion

1. B. D. Ehrman, *The Orthodox Corruption of Scripture: The Effect of Early Christological Controversies on the Text of the New Testament* (New York and Oxford: Oxford University Press, 1993).

2. J. Knust, 'Early Christian Re-Writing and the History of the *Pericope Adulterae*', *Journal of Early Christian Studies* 14 (2006), pp. 485–536.

BIBLIOGRAPHY

Aland, B., K. Aland, J. Karavidopoulos, C. M. Martini, and B. M. Metzger (eds), *Novum Testamentum Graece*, 27th edn, 8th (rev.) impression (Stuttgart: Deutsche Bibelgesellschaft, 2001).

Aland, K., M. Black, B. M. Metzger, and A. Wikren, *The Greek New Testament* (New York: United Bible Societies, 1966).

Aland, K., with M. Welte, B. Köster, and K. Junack, *Kurzgefasste Liste der griechischen Handschriften des Neuen Testaments*, Arbeiten zur Neutestamentlichen Text-forschung 1, 2nd edn (Berlin and New York: De Gruyter, 1994).

Aland, K.†, B. Aland, and K. Wachtel, with K. Witte (eds), *Text und Textwert der griechischen Handschriften des Neuen Testaments*, V: *Das Johannesevangelium*, Arbeiten zur Neutestamentlichen Textforschung 35–6 (Berlin and New York: De Gruyter, 2005).

Blomkvist, V., 'The Euthalian Apparatus: Text, Translation, Commentary' (University of Oslo, doctoral dissertation, 2011).

Bornkamm, G., G. Barth, and H. J. Held, *Überlieferung und Auslegung im Matthäusevangelium* (Neukirchen: Kreis Moers, 1960) [ET: *Tradition and Interpretation in Matthew* (London: SCM Press, 1963)].

Bover, J. M., *Novi Testamenti: Biblia Graeca et Latina* (Madrid: Consejo Superior de Investigaciones Científicas, 1943).

Bowers, F., *Textual and Literary Criticism* (Cambridge: Cambridge University Press, 1959).

Bowers, F., *Bibliography and Literary Criticism: The Lyell Lectures, Oxford, Trinity Term 1959* (Oxford: Clarendon Press, 1964).

British and Foreign Bible Society, *Η Καινή Διαθήκη*, 2nd edn (London: British and Foreign Bible Society, 1958).

Bultmann, R., *Die Geschichte der synoptischen Tradition* (Göttingen: Vandenhoek & Ruprecht, 1921) [ET: *The History of the Synoptic Tradition* (Oxford: Blackwell, 1963)].

Burton, P. H., H. A. G. Houghton, R. F. MacLachlan, and D. C. Parker (eds), *Vetus Latina: Die Reste der Altlateinischen Bibel nach Petrus Sabatier neu gesammelt und herausgegeben von der Erzabtei Beuron unter der Leitung von Roger Gryson*, 19: *Johannes* (Freiburg: Herder, 2011–).

Cockle, W. E. H. (ed.), Oxyrhynchus Papyrus 4499, in N. Gonis, J. Chapa, J. L. Martínez, et al. (eds), *The Oxyrhynchus Papyri*, vol. 66 (London: Egypt Exploration Fund, 1966), pp. 10–37.

Codex Sinaiticus: A Facsimile (London: British Library, and Peabody, MA: Hendrickson, 2010).

Colwell, E. C., 'Biblical Criticism: Lower and Higher', *Journal of Biblical Literature* 67 (1948), pp. 1–12.

Conzelmann, H., *Die Mitte der Zeit: Studien zur Theologie des Lukas* (Tübingen: Mohr, 1954) [ET: *The Theology of St Luke* (London: Faber & Faber, 1960)].

Cozza, J., *Sacrorum Bibliorum uetustissima fragmenta graeca et latina ex palimpsestis codicibus Bibliothecae Cryptoferratensis eruta, Pars 2* (Rome: Spithoever, 1867).

Dibelius, M., *Die Formgeschichte des Evangeliums* (Tübingen: Mohr (Siebeck), 1919) [ET: *From Tradition to Gospel* (London: Ivor Nicholson and Watson, 1934)].

Dyce, A. (ed.), *Richard Bentley: The Works*, vol. 3 (London, 1838; repr. Hildesheim and New York: Olms, 1971).

Ehrman, B. D., *The Orthodox Corruption of Scripture: The Effect of Early Christological Controversies on the Text of the New Testament* (New York and Oxford: Oxford University Press, 1993).

Elliott, J. K., *A Bibliography of Greek New Testament Manuscripts*, Society for New Testament Studies, Monograph Series 62, 2nd edn (Cambridge: Cambridge University Press, 2000).

Evans, C. A., 'Textual Criticism and Textual Confidence: How Reliable is Scripture?', in R. B. Stewart (ed.), *The Reliability of the New Testament: Bart D. Ehrman and Daniel B. Wallace in Dialogue* (Minneapolis: Fortress, 2011), pp. 161–72.

Fee, G. D., 'Codex Sinaiticus in the Gospel of John: A Contribution to Methodology in Establishing Textual Relationships', *New Testament Studies* 15 (1968), pp. 23–44.

Gäbel G., 'The Text of 𝔓 127 (P. Oxy. 4968) and its Relationship with the Text of Codex Bezae', *Novum Testamentum* 53 (2011), pp. 107–52.

Galen, Περὶ ᾿Αλυπησίας, Œuvres, vol. 4: *Ne pas se chagriner*, ed. and trans. V. Boudon-Millot and J. Jouanna, with A. Pietrobelli (Paris: Editions Belles Lettres, 2010).

Gamble, H.Y., *The Textual History of the Letter to the Romans*, Studies and Documents 42 (Grand Rapids: Eerdmans, 1977).

Gregory, C. R., *Textkritik des Neuen Testamentes*, 3 vols (Leipzig: J. C. Hinrichs, 1900–9).

Grenfell, B. P., and A. S. Hunt, *The Oxyrhynchus Papyri* (London: Egypt Exploration Fund, 1898–).

Η Καινη Διαθηκη. Novum Testamentum ex regiis aliisque optimis editionibus cum cura expressa (Leiden: Elzevir, 1633).

Holmes, M. W. (ed.), *The Greek New Testament: SBL Edition* (Atlanta: Society of Biblical Literature, and Bellingham, WA: Logos Bible Software, 2010).

Houghton, H. A. G., *Augustine's Text of John: Patristic Citations and Latin Gospel Manuscripts* (Oxford: Oxford University Press, 2008).

Jongkind, D., 'Some Observations on the Relevance of the "Early Byzantine Glossary" of Paul for the Textual Criticism of the *Corpus Paulinum*', *Novum Testamentum* 53 (2011), pp. 358–75.

Jordan, C. R. D., 'The Textual Tradition of the Gospel of John in Greek Gospel Lectionaries from the Middle Byzantine Period (8th–11th century)' (Birmingham University, unpublished PhD dissertation, 2010).

Kemp, B. J., *Ancient Egypt: Anatomy of a Civilization*, 2nd edn (London: Routledge, 2006).

Kenyon, F. G., *The Chester Beatty Biblical Papyri: Descriptions and Texts of the Twelve Manuscripts on Papyrus of the Greek Bible* (London: Emery Walker, 1934–7).

Knust, J., 'Early Christian Re-Writing and the History of the *Pericope Adulterae*', *Journal of Early Christian Studies* 14 (2006), pp. 485–536.

Lachmann, K., *Novum Testamentum Graece* (Berlin: Reimer, 1831).

Lachmann, K., *Novum Testamentum Graece et Latine*, 2 vols (Berlin: Reimer, 1842–50).

Lefebvre, G., 'Fragments grecs des Evangiles', *Bulletin de l'Institut français d'archéologie orientale* 4 (1905), pp. 1–15.

Legg, S. C. E., *Nouum Testamentum Graece secundum textum Westcotto-Hortianum, Euangelium secundum Marcum* (Oxford: Oxford University Press, 1935).

Legg, S. C. E., *Nouum Testamentum Graece secundum textum Westcotto-Hortianum, Euangelium secundum Matthaeum* (Oxford: Oxford University Press, 1940).

Lowden, J., *The Jaharis Gospel Lectionary: The Story of a Byzantine Book* (New York: The Metropolitan Museum of Art, and New Haven and London: Yale University Press, 2009).

Maas, P., *Textual Criticism* (Oxford: Oxford University Press, 1958) [Ger. original: *Textkritik*, 3rd edn (Leipzig: Teubner, 1957)].

McKendrick, S., *In a Monastery Library: Preserving Codex Sinaiticus and the Greek Written Heritage* (London: British Library, 2006).

Martin, V., *Papyrus Bodmer II: Evangile de Jean chap. 1–14* (Cologny-Geneva: Bibliotheca Bodmeriana, 1956).

Martin, V., *Papyrus Bodmer II: Supplément. Evangile de Jean chap. 14–21* (Cologny-Geneva: Bibliotheca Bodmeriana, 1958; rev. edn, with J. W. B. Barns, 1962).

Martin, V., and R. Kasser, *Papyrus Bodmer XIV: Evangile de Luc chap. 3–24* (Cologny-Geneva: Bibliotheca Bodmeriana, 1961).

Martin, V., and R. Kasser, *Papyrus Bodmer XV: Evangile de Jean chap. 1–15* (Cologny-Geneva: Bibliotheca Bodmeriana, 1961).

Matthaei, C. F., *Novum Testamentum Graece et Latine* (Riga, 1782–88).

Maxwell, K., 'The Afterlife of Texts: Decorative Style Manuscripts and New Testament Textual Criticism', in L. Jones (ed.), *Images and Afterlife: Essays in Honor of Annemarie Weyl Carr* (Aldershot: Ashgate Press, forthcoming).

Merk, A. (ed.), *Novum Testamentum Graece et Latine* (Rome: Pontifical Biblical Institute, 1933).

Metzger, B. M., *The Text of the New Testament: Its Transmission, Corruption, and Restoration* (New York: Oxford University Press, 1964).

Metzger, B. M., and B. D. Ehrman, *The Text of the New Testament: Its Transmission, Corruption, and Restoration*, 4th edn (Oxford: Oxford University Press, 2005).

Mill, J., *Η Καινή Διαθήκη* etc. (Oxford, 1707).

Mink, G. 'Contamination, Coherence, and Coincidence in Textual Transmission', in K. Wachtel and M. W. Holmes (eds), *The Textual History of the Greek New Testament: Changing Views in Contemporary Research*, Society of Biblical Literature, Text-Critical Studies 8 (Atlanta: Society of Biblical Literature, 2011), pp. 141–216.

Moulton, W. F., and A. S. Geden, *A Concordance to the Greek Testament* (Edinburgh, T. & T. Clark, 1897).

Murray, J. A. H., *A New English Dictionary on Historical Principles*, vol. 8 (Oxford: Clarendon Press, 1914).

Nelson, R. S., *Theodore Hagiopetrites: A Late Byzantine Scribe and Illuminator*, 2 vols, Veröffentlichungen der Kommission für Byzantinistik 4 (Vienna: Österreichische Akademie der Wissenschaften, 1991).

Nestle, E. (ed.), *Novum Testamentum Graece* (Stuttgart: Deutsche Bibelgesellschaft, 1898).

Nestle, E., *Einführung in das griechische Neue Testament*, 4th edn, rev. E. von Dobschütz, (Göttingen: Vandenhoeck & Ruprecht, 1923).

Nestle-Aland, *Novum Testamentum Graece,* see B. Aland, K. Aland, J. Karavidopoulos, C. M. Martini, and B. M. Metzger (eds) (2001).

The New Testament in Greek III: The Gospel According to St. Luke, Edited by the American and British Committees of the International Greek New Testament Project, 2 vols (Oxford: Oxford University Press, 1984–7).

Nicklas, T., and T. Wasserman, 'Theologische Linien im *Codex Bodmer Miscellani*? [*sic*]', in T. J. Kraus and T. Nicklas (eds), *New Testament Manuscripts: Their Texts and their World*, Texts and Editions for New Testament Study 2 (Leiden: Brill, 2006), pp. 161–88.

Novum Testamentum Graecum: Editio critica maior, ed. Institut für Neutestamentliche Textforschung, IV: *Die Katholischen Briefe*, ed. B. Aland, K. Aland†, G. Mink, H., Strutwolf, and K. Wachtel (Stuttgart: Deutsche Bibelgesellschaft, 1997–2005).

Parker, D. C., *Codex Bezae: An Early Christian Manuscript and its Text* (Cambridge: Cambridge University Press, 1992).

Parker, D. C., *The Living Text of the Gospels* (Cambridge: Cambridge University Press, 1997).

Parker, D. C. *An Introduction to the New Testament Manuscripts and their Texts* (Cambridge: Cambridge University Press, 2008).

Parker, D. C., *Codex Sinaiticus: The Story of the World's Oldest Bible* (London: British Library, and Peabody, MA: Hendrikson, 2010).

Parker, D. C., 'Is "Living Text" Compatible with "Initial Text"? Editing the Gospel of John', in K. Wachtel and M. W. Holmes (eds), *The Textual History of the Greek New Testament: Changing Views in Contemporary Research*, Society of Biblical Literature, Text-Critical Studies 8 (Atlanta: Society of Biblical Literature, 2011), pp. 13–21.

Parker, D. C., U. B. Schmid, and W. J. Elliott (eds), *The New Testament in Greek IV: The Gospel According to St. John, Edited by the American and British Committees of the International Greek New Testament Project*, vol. 2: *The Majuscules*, New Testament Tools, Studies and Documents 37 (Leiden: E. J. Brill, 2007).

Parker, D. C., and S. R. Pickering (eds), Oxyrhynchus Papyrus 4968, in D. Leith, D. C. Parker, S. R. Pickering, et al. (eds), *The Oxyrhynchus Papyri*, vol. 74 (London: Egypt Exploration Fund, 2009).

Pervo, R. I., *Profit with Delight: The Literary Genre of the Acts of the Apostles* (Philadelphia: Fortress Press, 1987).

Pickering, S. R., 'The Significance of Non-Continuous New Testament Textual Materials in Papyri', in D. G. K. Taylor (ed.), *Studies in the Early Text of the Gospels and Acts*, Text and Studies Third Series 1 (Birmingham: Birmingham University Press, 1999), pp. 121–41.

Porter, S. E., 'Textual Criticism in the Light of Diverse Textual Evidence for the Greek New Testament: An Expanded Proposal', in T. J. Kraus and T. Nicklas (eds), *New Testament Manuscripts: Their Texts and their World*, Texts and Editions for New Testament Study 2 (Leiden: Brill, 2006), pp. 305–37.

Puech, E., 'Le tombeau de Siméon et Zacharie dans la vallée de Josaphat', *Revue Biblique* 111 (2004), pp. 563–77.

Reuss, J., *Matthäus-, Markus- u. Johannes-Katenen nach den handschriftlichen Quellen untersucht*, Neutestamentliche Abhandlungen 18/4–5 (Münster: Aschendorf, 1941).

Revised English Bible (Oxford: Oxford University Press, and Cambridge: Cambridge University Press, 1989).

Römer, C. E., 'Ostraka mit christlichen Texten aus der Sammlung Flinders Petrie', *Zeitschrift für Papyrologie und Epigraphik* 145 (2003), pp. 183–201.

Schmidt, K. L., *Der Rahmen der Geschichte Jesu: Literarkritische Untersuchungen zur ältesten Jesusüberlieferung* (Berlin: Trowitzsch, 1919).

Scrivener, F. H. A., *A Plain Introduction to the Criticism of the New Testament for the Use of Biblical Students*, 2 vols, 4th edn, rev. E. Miller (London and New York: George Bell, and Cambridge: Deighton Bell, 1894).

The Shorter Oxford English Dictionary on Historical Principles, rev. C. T. Onions (Oxford: Clarendon Press, 1973).

Skeat, T. C., 'The Codex Sinaiticus, the Codex Vaticanus and Constantine', *Journal of Theological Studies* 50 (1999), pp. 583–625; repr. in J. K. Elliott (ed.), *The Collected Biblical Writings of T. C. Skeat*, Supplements to Novum Testamentum 113 (Leiden and Boston: E. J. Brill, 2004), pp. 193–237.

Souter, A. (ed.) *Novum Testamentum Graece: Textvi a retractatoribus anglis adhibito brevem adnotationem criticam svbiecit* (Oxford: Clarendon Press, 1910).

Streeter, B. H., *The Four Gospels: A Study of Origins Treating of the Manuscript Tradition, Sources, Authorship, & Dates* (London: Macmillan, 1924).

Timpanaro, S., *The Genesis of Lachmann's Method*, ed. and tr. G. W. Most (Chicago and London: University of Chicago Press, 2005) [It. original: *La genesi del metodo del Lachmann*, 2nd edn (Turin: Liviana Editrice, 1981)].

Tischendorf, C., *Bibliorum Codex Sinaiticus Petropolitanus*, 4 vols (Leipzig: Giesecke & Devrient, 1862).

Tischendorf, C., *Novum Testamentum Graece... Editio octava critica maior*, vols 1–2: text (Leipzig: J. C. Hinrichs, 1869–72); vol. 3: *Prolegomena*, by C. R. Gregory (Leipzig: J. C. Hinrichs, 1884).

Tregelles, S. P., *The Greek New Testament* (London: Bagster/Stewart, 1857–79).

United Bible Societies, *The Greek New Testament*, see K. Aland, M. Black, B. M. Metzger, and A. Wikren (eds) (1966).

Vogel, M., and V. Gardthausen, *Die griechischen Schreiber des Mittelalters und der Renaissance* (Leipzig: Harrassowitz, 1909; repr. Hildesheim: Georg Olms, 1966).

Von Soden, H., *Die Schriften des Neuen Testaments in ihrer ältesten erreichbaren Textgestalt hergestellt auf Grund ihrer Textgeschichte*, 3 vols (Berlin: Arthur Glaue, 1902–7).

Wachtel, K. and M. W. Holmes (eds), *The Textual History of the Greek New Testament: Changing Views in Contemporary Research*, Society of Biblical Literature Text-Critical Studies 8 (Atlanta: Society of Biblical Literature, 2011).

Wasserman, T., 'Papyrus 72 and the *Bodmer Miscellaneous Codex*', *New Testament Studies* 51 (2005), pp. 137–54.

Wasserman, T., *The Epistle of Jude: Its Text and Transmission*, Coniectanea Biblica, New Testament Series, 43 (Lund: Almqvist & Wiksell International, 2006).

Wasserman, T., 'P[78] (P. Oxy. XXXIV 2684)—The Epistle of Jude on an Amulet?', in T. J. Kraus and T. Nicklas (eds), *New Testament Manuscripts: Their Texts and their World*, Texts and Editions for New Testament Study 2 (Leiden: E. J. Brill, 2006), pp. 137–60.

Westcott, B. F., and F. J. A. Hort, *The New Testament in the Original Greek*, 2 vols (London: Macmillan, 1881).

Weyl Carr, Annemarie, *Byzantine Illumination, 1150–1250: The Study of a Provincial Tradition* (Chicago: University of Chicago Press, 1987).

Willard, L. C., *A Critical Study of the Euthalian Apparatus*, Arbeiten zur neutesta-mentlichen Textforschung 41 (Berlin and New York: De Gruyter, 2009).

Zacagni, L.A., *Collectanea Monumentorum Veterum Ecclesiae ... 4 Euthalii Episc. Sulcensis Actuum Apostolorum, & quatuordecim S. Pauli, aliarumque septem Catholicarum episto-larum editio ...*(Rome: Sacrae Congregationis de Propaganda Fide, 1698).

Zuntz, G., *The Text of the Epistles: A Disquisition upon the Corpus Paulinum*, The Schweich Lectures 1946 (London: The British Academy, 1953).

INDEX OF MANUSCRIPTS

London, British Library (*Cont.*)
  Add. Ms. 43725 (Codex Sinaiticus,
  Gregory-Aland 01) 29, 38, 40,
  47–8, 62, 73–4, 81, 83, 92–3, 94, 96
  n.45, 107, 108, 115, 133, 134–6, 147
  Burney 21 (Gregory-Aland 484) 70–1
  Or. 5707 *see* Cairo, Egyptian
  Museum 9239
  Royal Ms. 1 D.V-VIII (Codex
  Alexandrinus, Gregory-Aland
  02) 38, 53, 62

Moscow, Historical Museum V.29,
  S. 119 *see* Athens, National
  Library 1371
Munich, Bayerische Staatsbibliothek
  Gr. 465 (Gregory-Aland 427)
  54 n.46
Munich, Stadtbibliothek
  Cod. ms. 191 52
Munich, Universitätsbibliothek
  2° Cod. ms. 30 (Gregory-Aland
  033) 43, 47–50

New Haven, Yale University, Beinecke
  Library Dura Pg. 24 (formerly P.
  Dura 24) (Gregory-Aland 0212) 39
New York, Metropolitan Museum of Art
  2007.286 (Jaharis Gospel Lection-
  ary) (Gregory-Aland L351) 55, 59
  Department of Egyptian Art 14.1.527
  (Gregory-Aland P44) 33 n.1

Oxford, Ashmolean Museum
  Papyrus Oxyrhynchus 2684
  (Gregory-Aland P78) 35, 37
  Papyrus Oxyrhynchus 4499
  (Gregory-Aland P115) 108
  Papyrus Oxyrhynchus 4968
  (Gregory-Aland P127) 108

Oxford, Bodleian Library
  Canon.Gr. 34 (Gregory-Aland
  522) 92
  Clarendon Press b. 2, fols 12–19, 26
  see London, British Library Add.
  34274
Oxford, Christ Church, Wake 2 *see*
  Athens, National Library 1371

Paris, Bibliothèque Nationale de
  France
  Coislin Gr. 199 (Gregory-Aland
  35) 19 n.17
  Copt. 129, 7, fol. 35 etc.
  (Gregory-Aland 029) 47–9
  Copt. 129, 7, fol. 72, 129,8 etc.
  see London, British Library Add.
  Ms. 34274
  Gr. 9 (Gregory-Aland 04) 47–9
  Gr. 14 (Gregory-Aland 33) 49–50
  Gr. 47 (Gregory-Aland 18) 19 n.17,
  89–90, 98
  Gr. 62 (Gregory-Aland 019) 47–50
  Gr. 212 (Gregory-Aland 317) 47–8
  Lat. 11533 39 n.13
Patmos, Ioannou 58 (Gregory-Aland
  1160) 33 n.2
Poitiers, Bibliothèque Municipale 17
  (65) (Old Latin 39) 56 n.49

Rio de Janeiro, Biblioteca Nacionale
  I.2 (Gregory-Aland 2437)
  136 n.9
Rome, Biblioteca Vallicelliana E.40
  (Gregory-Aland 397) 47–50

St Petersburg, National Library of
  Russia
  Gr. 10 (Gregory-Aland 083) 47, 49
  Gr. 53 (Gregory-Aland 565) 76

St Petersburg, Russian Academy,
  Collection of the Russian
  Institute of Constantinople 165
  (Gregory-Aland 2267) 33 n.2

Tirana, State Archive Beratinus 2
  (Gregory-Aland 1143) 76

Vatican, Vatican Library
  Barb. gr. 495 (Gregory-Aland
    849) 45 n.31, 47–51
  Barb. gr. 504 (Gregory-Aland
    850) 45 n.31, 50 n.41
  Barb. gr. 521, fol. 7-391 (Gregory-
    Aland 392) 43 n.27
  Borg. gr. Copt. 109 (Gregory-Aland
    029) 47–8
  Ottob. gr. 432 (Gregory-Aland
    391) 43 n.24
  Vat. gr. 592 (Gregory-Aland
    1819) 45 n.31, 51 n.42
  Vat. gr. 593 (Gregory-Aland
    1820) 45 n.31
  Vat. gr. 644 (Gregory-Aland 856) 70–1
  Vat. gr. 1610 46
  Vat. gr. 1618 (Gregory-Aland
    377) 43 n.26
  Vat. gr. 1209 (Codex Vaticanus,
    Gregory-Aland 03) 45, 47–9,
    73–4, 81, 83, 90, 92–3, 107,
    108, 147
  Vat. gr. 1472 (Gregory Aland
    865) 49–50
Vendôme, Bibliothèque Municipale 2
  (Old Latin 40) 56 n.49
Venice, Biblioteca Nazionale Marciana
  Gr. I.19 (1416) (Gregory-Aland
    412) 70–2
  Gr. Z.121 (324) (Gregory-Aland
    2129) 45 n.31, 51 n.42

Gr. Z. 546 (786) (Gregory-Aland
  617) 88–91
Verona, Biblioteca Capitolare LI (49)
  (Old Latin 49) 53–4
Vienna, Österreichische
  Nationalbibliothek
  P. 2312 35, 37
  Pap. K. 15.2699.2700.9007.9031
    see London, British Library Add.
    Ms. 34274
  Pap. K 8706 (Gregory-Aland
    P42) 52–3
  Theol. gr. 302, fols 1–353 (Gregory-
    Aland 424) 91

Washington, Freer Gallery of Art
  06.274 (Gregory-Aland 032,
    032S) 47–9, 110

2 Concordance of Gregory-Aland Numbers

P42 Vienna, Österreichische National-
  bibliothek Pap. K 8706
P44 New York, Metropolitan Museum
  of Art, Department of Egyptian
  Art 14.1.527
P45 Dublin, Chester Beatty Collection
  P. Chester Beatty I
P46 Dublin, Chester Beatty Collection
  P. Chester Beatty II
P47 Dublin, Chester Beatty Collection
  P. Chester Beatty III
P66 Cologny-Geneva, Bibliotheca
  Bodmeriana P. Bodmer II
P72 Cologny-Geneva, Bibliotheca
  Bodmeriana P. Bodmer VII, VIII
P75 Cologny-Geneva, Bibliotheca
  Bodmeriana P. Bodmer XIV-V
P78 Oxford, Ashmolean Museum
  Papyrus Oxyrhynchus 2684

3 Concordance of Old Latin Numbers

INDEX OF NAMES AND SUBJECTS

Printed in Great Britain
by Amazon

18638046R00112